The Illustrated History of
MANCHESTER'S SUBURBS

GLYNIS COOPER

The Illustrated History of

MANCHESTER'S SUBURBS

GLYNIS COOPER

Published in association with Manchester Libraries

MANCHESTER CITY COUNCIL

LIBRARIES & THEATRES

breedon **books**

PUBLISHING

First published in Great Britain in 2002 by
The Breedon Books Publishing Company Limited
Breedon House, 3 The Parker Centre,
Derby, DE21 4SZ.

Dedication

Dedicated to my family whose roots lie in the Manchester millscapes and to Mike Greenman without whom this book would not have been written.

ISBN 1 85983 292 X

Printed and bound by Butler & Tanner, Frome, Somerset, England.

Cover printing by Lawrence-Allen Colour Printers,
Weston-super-Mare, Somerset.

Contents

MANCHESTER ARCHIVES AND LOCAL STUDIES, MANCHESTER CENTRAL LIBRARY

The pictures in this book are all taken from **the Manchester Computerised Local Image Collection**, which includes over 77,000 images covering the history of Manchester's development from the 18th century to the present day. The originals are mainly photographs but there are also prints, drawings, watercolour paintings and postcards.

Thanks in part to a major award from the Heritage Lottery Fund, the entire collection of 77,000 plus images can be viewed on computers situated in the Local Studies Library section of Manchester Archives and Local Studies. Each of the images can be enlarged to full-screen size, and can be printed as a laser print. In the future, it is hoped that resources will be found to mount the whole collection on the Internet. At present, there is a small collection of 200 plus images which can be seen via our website, www.manchester.gov.uk/libraries/arls, by selecting the link 'Local Image Collection'.

The collection as a whole contains street scenes, buildings, general views, pictures of people as individuals, or groups, and events and activities portraying the history of the area. Strongly represented are images of the Industrial Revolution and its effects on the lives of the city's population. In addition, the collection contains an almost complete street-by-street photographic survey of the city for the period 1950–1970, a key period in the post-war redevelopment of the city.

Manchester Archives and Local Studies has many other sources for the history of Manchester and the surrounding area. These include books – both reference and lending – maps, newspapers, also archives for a wide range of local organisations such as churches and businesses. Many of these sources are available in microfilm form. More details of our collections and how they can be accessed can be found on our website. Alternatively, please write or telephone.

Manchester Archives and Local Studies, Central Library, St Peter's Square, Manchester M2 5PD

Tel. 0161 234 1979, or 0161 234 1980 (archives only)

www.manchester.gov.uk/libraries/arls

N
W
E
S
BLACKLEY
CRUMPSALL
MOSTON
COLLY HURST
HARPURHEY
CHEETHAM
NEWTON HEATH
ANCOATS
MILES PLATTING
CLAYTON
CITY CENTRE
BESWICK
CHORLTON ON MEDLOCK
OPENSHAW
BRADFORD
ARDWICK
HULME
LONGSIGHT
GORTON
MOSS SIDE
VIC PARK
RUSHOLME
WHALLEY RANGE
FALLOWFIELD
CHORLTON CUM HARDY
LEVENSHULME
WITHINGTON
DIDSBURY
BURNAGE
NORTHENDEN
WYTHENSHAWE
MANCHESTER'S SUBURBS
Not to scale

Introduction

In the novel *Coningsby*, by Benjamin Disraeli, Coningsby says to a companion 'What would I not give to see Athens?' 'I have seen it,' replies his companion. 'The Age of Ruins is past. Have you seen Manchester? Manchester is as great a human exploit as Athens.'

Disraeli, renowned Victorian politician and prime minister turned novelist in his spare time, was paying Manchester the ultimate compliment. He had recognised the tremendous effort and the extraordinary circumstances which, within the space of a single century, had turned a modest English country town into the industrial centre of the world.

Today Manchester has a population of over two and a half million people, plus a further seven million living in Greater Manchester. It is split in to three parts: the city of Manchester, the suburbs of Manchester, and the surrounding area known as Greater Manchester. The city is the heart of Manchester and includes the areas around Piccadilly, Market Street, St Ann's Square, Deansgate and Castlefield. There are 30 townships, or suburbs, surrounding the city: Ancoats; Ardwick; Beswick; Blackley; Bradford; Burnage; Cheetham; Chorlton-cum-Hardy; Chorlton on Medlock; Clayton; Collyhurst; Crumpsall; Didsbury; Fallowfield; Gorton; Harpurhey; Hulme; Levenshulme; Longsight; Miles Platting; Moss Side; Moston; Newton Heath; Northenden; Openshaw; Rusholme; Victoria Park; Whalley Range; Withington/Ladybarn and Wythenshawe. Greater Manchester surrounds the townships and covers Trafford; Salford; Wigan; Bolton; Bury; Rochdale; Oldham; Tameside and Stockport. It is the largest industrial conurbation in the world, stretching for over 40 miles.

A description of Manchester in 1725 by William Stukely states that the town was 'placed between two rivers, having rocky and precipitous banks.' The rivers in question are the Irwell and the Medlock. Between the confluence of the two rivers was contained the Roman fort at Castlefield, what is now the area of Market Street and Deansgate, and Hanging Ditch. Hanging Ditch, at the point where the River Irk joins the River Irwell, is about 120ft wide and 40ft deep, a fissure running through the outcrop of red sandstone on which the original settlement was situated. Records of a bridge at that point go back to at least 1422 and it is probable that there was a bridge there long before that. The hill, partially protected by two rivers, and with a ready water supply, was ideal for settlement. In prehistory (i.e. before the Romans) England was heavily wooded and the hill would have been an excellent lookout as well as being easier to defend than a flat site. Celia Fiennes, visiting in 1697, noted that 'there is a large church, all stone, and standeth so high that, walking around the church yard you see the whole town.'

Early peoples were quick to recognise the benefits offered by the hill partially surrounded by rivers. It was home to Stone Age, Bronze Age and Iron Age people. They left behind their stone, flint and bronze tools, weapons and jewellery on the banks of the rivers. The names Irwell (winding stream) and Irk (wandering) are of Latin derivation and may have been bestowed by the Romans, but the Medlock (meadow stream) took its name from the Celts who inhabited Britain from around 500 BC and never left. That the Celts settled in Manchester is not in doubt. It has been said that it is surprising that there has been a lack of Celtic finds in the area of the Roman fort at Castlefield, where the Irwell and the Medlock meet just 'two fly shottes' (John Leland, in his *Itinerary* of 1540) from the sandstone outcrop, but that is not where the Celts would have chosen to live. The sandstone outcrop would have been their home and artefact finds support this theory. A hill in woodlands and very close to water was the Celtic ideal of a desirable residence and indeed they gave Manchester its original name of Mamcestre: formed from *mam* meaning hill and *ceastre* meaning walled town. Their settlement would have been on top of the sandstone outcrop and fortified by a ring of wooden posts or a wooden fence. The Castlefield site meets more of the Roman criteria for fortified settlement plus of course the fact the Celtic tribe of the Brigantes (who held sway in northern England at that time) were firmly in control of the nearby high ground. The fort at Castlefield was built by Agricola in around AD 70 and was occupied for three centuries. The Romans had a love-hate relationship with the Brigantes but never quite got the better of them. The Brigantes knew their territory and practised guerrilla warfare, which the Romans, with their precise military ways, were not trained to handle. On the other hand, the Brigantes, to use a modern idiom, were not above making a fast buck, and traded with the Romans when they were not fighting them. The Celtic Brigantian queen, Cartimandua, thoroughly fed up with her husband, got rid of him by betraying him to the Romans. When the Romans finally abandoned Manchester during the 'long sunset' the Celts simply reclaimed their territory, but not for long.

In AD 620 there was a Saxon invasion from the north-east kingdom of Deira. Saxon soldiers, under the leadership of Edwin, king of Northumbria, swept down through the Pennines via the Longdendale Valley and attacked Manchester. The Saxons better understood the fighting ways of the Celts and savagely defeated them on a number of occasions. The major contribution of the Saxon people was to settle most of the townships and villages around Manchester which, over a thousand years later, would grow and unite to make Manchester the international home of the cotton industry. Back in 800 however, there were quite different problems to face. Fierce warriors in their long boats were sailing across the northern seas, invading the countryside and causing widespread panic with the ferocity of their attacks. By 870 they had reached the Manchester region. In desperation the Saxon settlers sought to defend themselves by building a defensive earthwork to try and protect their small villages. It stretched from Ashton to Chorlton, a distance of some six or seven miles. The villages survived, unlike most of the Saxons, and the area came under the Danelaw for a while. During the early 900s King Alfred (of burnt cakes fame) and his son, Edward the Elder, managed to reunite most of England, wresting much of the power from the Danes. According to the *Anglo-Saxon Chronicle*, in 923 Edward took possession of Manchester, effected repairs to the town and garrisoned it. Sometime later, in the 10th century, the church of St Mary (which in later centuries would become the cathedral) was founded. It became a collegiate church in 1421 and was dedicated to St Mary, St Denys and St George by Henry V.

The Norman Conquest of 1066 was responsible for Manchester becoming a barony and in 1086, the year of the Domesday Book (in which the church of St Mary received a brief mention), Manchester became a possession of the Grelly family and remained so until 1309. The barony comprised the demesne manor of Manchester and Withington manor (both of which included all the settlements that would eventually become Manchester suburbs, except the Cheshire trio of Northenden, Northenden Etchells and Baguley; the latter two now being encompassed by Wythenshawe); Salford manor, Barton-on-Irwell manor, Ashton manor, Heaton Norris manor and lands around Horwich. The foundations of Manchester, as it is known today, had been laid. The manor house for Manchester stood where Chetham's School of Music stands near Victoria Station, with kitchen gardens sloping away down towards the Irk and the Irwell. There was a deer park out at Blackley. A mill for grinding corn stood on Long Millgate and tenants had to pay for the privilege of using it. There was also a communal oven for baking bread near the mill and, again, tenants had to use it and pay for the privilege. Flax was grown locally for linen, the weaving of which was a cottage industry, as was the spinning of woollen yarn. According to the *Survey of the Manor of Manchester* in 1322 there was also a fulling mill (for the cleansing of cloth and leather) by the Irk.

Every three weeks the Court Baron met in Manchester. It was a kind of superior magistrates court and here the Grellys and lords of the other manors within the barony met and sat as 'judges' or 'doomsmen'. Penalties, however, must have been somewhat harsher than today since the lord could 'claim the liberty of the gallows, the pit, the pillory and the tumbril.' To add to the lack of political correctness a 'grith' (bailiff) and four foot bailiffs would forcibly carry out the sentence of the court.

A market was held every Saturday and in 1227 Henry III granted the Grellys the right to hold an annual fair each September on Acresfield, which today is St Ann's Square and the surrounding area. After the fair had finished the land was available for common grazing. By 1282 tenants of the Manchester manor were exempt from the customary compulsory agricultural labour which those on other manors had to render to their lords, and they had their own court, the Portmoot. A charter, whose 34 clauses would regulate local government until 1846, was granted in 1301 to the inhabitants of Manchester by Thomas Grelly, the last of the Grelly line, and in 1309 the barony passed to the de la Warre family. Sir

Nicholas Mosley, knighted in 1599, bought the manor of Manchester and governed it through a Court Leet, which controlled fairs and markets, regulated the prices of bread and ale, and meted out punishments to miscreants. Manchester declared itself firmly on the side of the Parliamentarians during the Civil War and in 1654 sent its first Member of Parliament to the House of Commons. The town was incorporated as a borough in 1838 and became a city in 1853.

The Tudor traveller and writer, John Leland, waxed lyrical about Manchester in his *Itinerary* of 1540, describing the place as 'the fairest, best buildid, quikkest and most populous tounne of all Lancastreshire... there be divers stone bridges... but the best of three arches is over Irwel... on this bridge is a praty little chapel (pretty little chantry chapel which later became a prison)... on Hirke (Irk) river be divers faire mills...'.

Nearly 200 years later, in 1724, William Stukely in his *Itinerarium Curiosum* continues this theme: '...Manchester... the largest, most rich, populous, and busy village in England having about 2,400 families... they have looms which work twenty four laces at once, which were stolen from the Dutch...'. Stukely probably meant borrowed or copied, rather than stolen, since he was writing barely 20 years after the death of the Dutch King William III who reigned on the English throne for 13 years.

Flemish workers and Huguenots who had fled their French and Belgian homelands in Tudor times, because of religious persecution, settled in the north of England. They had brought their weaving skills with them and perhaps it was they who set Manchester on course to become the textile capital of the world. In 1552 an Act was passed to control the quality of Manchester cottons, and during the 1580s came the first accolade to Manchester's textile trade from William Camden who wrote that Manchester became 'in the last age much more famous for its manufacture of stuffs called Manchester cottons...'

The first exchange was built in Manchester market place by the then lord of the manor, Sir Oswald Mosley, in 1729, and also housed the Court Leet. It was here that all manner of trading was carried on. Jonathan Aiken, who wrote *A description of the countryside for thirty to forty miles around Manchester* in 1790, made a study of the textile trade as it was in the 1770s/1780s. He estimated the annual cotton trade in 1770 to be worth around £200,000 (just under £11 million today). By this time cotton was being imported from the East Indies and there were different types of cotton manufacture such as candlewick, hosiery, silk and linen, fustian, calico and muslin. 'Chapmen' took goods via packhorse to sell all over the country, returning with packs of sheep wool for worsted yarn makers in Manchester and Rochdale. Unsold goods were kept at local inns and hostelries. It was small-scale merchandising from which grew the large-scale merchandising of the late 18th and 19th centuries. Merchants warehouses became a familiar sight around the city and many still survive today. The largest and best known is that of S. & J. Watts on Portland Street, where each floor was built in a different architectural style. It opened in 1858 as 'the original cash and carry', and is now the Britannia Hotel, a Grade II listed building. Edmund Potter, grandfather of the internationally renowned children's writer, Beatrix Potter, had his warehouse at 14 Mosley Street in a four-storey red brick building which is currently home to Lloyds Bank; and her uncle, Crompton Potter, had a warehouse at 10 Charlotte Street which now houses (appropriately enough) a bookshop.

There was another side to this success story however. In his descriptions of Manchester, Aiken writes of dunghills on the roads, the lack of street lighting, infested dirty beds in lodging houses, and hot baths which cost today's equivalent of £11 each! During the latter half of the 18th century came the inventions that turned Manchester into a millscape: John Kay's fly shuttle in 1733 which doubled the speed and scope of weaving; James Hargreaves's spinning-jenny in 1764 which meant that 100 threads could be spun by one wheel; Richard Arkwright's water frame in 1769; Samuel Crompton's spinning mule in 1779 which produced fine, strong, even threads; and Edmund Cartwright's power loom in 1785. The first textile mills were built in the late 1770s and by the end of the century Aiken wrote of the 'prevalence of fevers of persons employed in the cotton mills.' The population explosion had also begun. At Christmas 1773 Aiken gives the population of Manchester as 22,481. By Christmas 1778, just five years later, figures had almost doubled to 42,821. It was the beginning of the end for Manchester as a country town and for the surrounding villages as pretty rural farming areas.

The rest, as they say, is history. Manchester and its suburbs were swept up by a technological revolution the like of which had not been seen before. For the suburbs life changed forever and their individual stories are chronicled in this book. For Manchester the city crackled with energy and creativity and prosperity in the 19th century. The building of the new Town Hall on Albert Square in 1877, to replace the old one which had stood on the corner of King Street and Cross Street since 1825, symbolised the pride and innovation and wealth of the city. A new exchange (now the Royal Exchange since receiving the royal assent in 1851), accommodating up to 11,000 dealers, was built in 1866 on Cross Street, near Cross Street Chapel where the Revd William Gaskell, husband of novelist Elizabeth Gaskell, preached, and where the Literary and Philosophical Society (founded in 1781) met. The Free Trade Hall was built in 1856 on Peter Street to commemorate the repeal of the Corn Laws achieved by the Anti-Corn Law League founded in 1838 by Manchester men Richard Cobden and John Bright. The original Free Trade Hall had been built of wood in 1840 as a venue for the well-attended debates on the Corn Laws when Manchester became associated with the principles of free trade. The *Manchester Guardian*, now known as the national newspaper, *The Guardian*, was founded in 1821 by John Edward Taylor. Mill owners, merchants and other persons of local prominence subscribed to the foundation of the Portico Library in 1806 on Charlotte Street. The library survives but it is not a public library and an annual subscription charge is still levied. The Portico is reminiscent of a 19th-century gentleman's club and has a dining room where good traditional English lunches are served to members only. John Rylands, a merchant and philanthropist, became Manchester's first self-made millionaire and the John Rylands Library was established on Deansgate in his memory by his widow after his death in 1888. The first Mechanics Institute in the country was opened in 1824. This subsequently became a Technical School in 1883 and UMIST in 1918, the oldest technical university in Britain. John Dalton, a chemist who discovered colour blindness, worked at Manchester New College on Mosley Street, and first put forward the atomic theory in his *New System of Chemical Philosophy*, published in 1810.

There was of course a downside to the reign of cotton as king. The poverty and appalling conditions which workers, particularly the navvies who built the railway and the canal networks of Manchester, had to endure reduced people like Frederick Engels and Elizabeth Gaskell to despair. Many lived in cellars which 'consisted of two rooms... each nine to ten feet square... some inhabited by ten persons or more...' Cholera was rife and there was an 'unwholesome, filthy and disease-engendering condition of the more confined and pauperised districts of the town'. There was also a report in 1832 by Dr Kay which stated that '...privvies are in a most disgraceful state, inaccessible from filth and too few for accommodation of the number of people...' and in Parliament Street there was 'one privvie in a narrow passage to serve 380 inhabitants...' In some parts of Manchester there was a programme of slum clearance in place as early as the 1880s. The Cotton Famine of the 1860s (as a result of the American Civil War) caused near starvation for thousands. Wealth was extremely unevenly distributed. Socialism flourished and so too did the trades unions. Marx and Engels did the research for their Communist Manifesto (published in 1848) in Chetham's Library near Victoria Station, the 'first free public library in the world'. The library had over 100,000 volumes.

There was a great need for political reform since the vast majority of Manchester's newly enlarged population had no proper representation in Parliament. A meeting at which well-known orators like Henry Hunt were to debate this issue was held on 8 January 1819 in St Peter's Fields, now St Peter's Street. A huge crowd numbering tens of thousands gathered. With memories of the French Revolution in 1789 still fresh in their minds the authorities panicked and called in the militia. Flags with revolutionary slogans were waved and the order was given for the troops to be sent in. Armed cavalry charged into the crowd slashing wildly with their sabres. The resulting carnage resembled a battlefield, prompting a comparison with Waterloo, and immortalising the tragedy as the Peterloo Massacre.

Near to Victoria Station is a statue of Robert Owen (1771–1858), a mill owner who lived in the house that had been built for Thomas de Quincy in Greenheys, and who fought almost single-handedly to prevent young children (under nine) being forced to work in the mills. Equal opportunities did not exist either and the Suffragette movement, led by Emmeline and Christabel Pankhurst, gathered momentum during the 1890s and 1900s, although the vote was not granted to everyone until 1928. Women lived, worked and died in unimaginably awful circumstances under the shadow of the mills. Although Manchester had built a great wealth for queen, country and empire, there had been a terrible price to pay.

Manchester suffered during World War One, the Depression of the 1930s and the Blitz of World War Two. By the 1960s the age of cotton was over and the Royal Exchange ceased trading in December 1968. The building now houses an innovative steel and glass 'theatre in the round', but the last trading figures are left in situ as a poignant reminder. Third World imports terminally undermined the British textile industry and Manchester was simply regarded by the rest of the country as a rather wet and mucky place full of derelict mills, their endless windows like sightless eyes of broken glass; mere shadows of the 'dark Satanic mills', those huge blackened hulks of buildings which had dominated the landscape, belching smoke that blotted out the sky and any hopes the workers might have entertained of a halfway decent life. However, as the stories of the suburbs show, there was a determination for this not to be the end. Modern industry, like ICI and ICL, moved in. Regeneration and redevelopment schemes were put into operation. High-rise flats and new shopping centres were built, and the Arndale Centre created as a pioneering venture. Old buildings took on a new lease of life. The Printworks became a shopping and cinema complex. Central Station is now the G-MEX centre. The Halle Orchestra moved from the Free Trade Hall to the new Bridgewater Hall opposite the G-MEX. Plays were premiered at the Royal Exchange Theatre before going down to London. An area near China Town, known as The Village, has become a cultural centre for alternative lifestyles. Pavement cafés appeared by the side of cleaned-up canals. Metrolink provided a new tram service for the 21st century. Then, in June 1996, an IRA bomb blew the heart out of Manchester.

Miraculously no one was killed or even seriously injured. Central government did its best to ignore what had happened. After a week the *Manchester Evening News* ran a banner headline 'Why will no one come to see us?' asking why no one of note had been to visit Manchester to assess the disaster as would have happened in London or other towns and cities. Eventually Michael Heseltine came and was visibly shocked by what he saw. He promised immediate aid. Since then Manchester has never looked back. Damaged buildings have been demolished, streets cleared, the last of the broken glass swept away. The city centre has been rebuilt. New businesses have moved in. Amid the modern developments of glass, steel and chrome, the Wellington Inn, a crooked brown and white timbered building, stands as a reminder of old Manchester long before the reign of King Cotton. The inn, together with the famous Sinclairs Oyster Bar and Shambles Square, has been moved just over a hundred metres to a new location off Exchange Square, while the former Corn Exchange near Victoria Station has become a new shopping centre known as the Triangle.

In the summer of 2002 Manchester will host the Commonwealth Games in a brand new sports stadium. Art and culture have been rejuvenated by a large multicultural population. Manchester Central Library, an unusual and completely circular four-storey building, opened in 1934, houses a special Chinese Library on its second floor. China Town, near the Britannia Hotel, is entered via a beautiful Chinese Arch 'symbolising peace, health and prosperity'. Museums like the Pumphouse and the Museum of Science and Industry serve to promote Manchester's unique heritage and its place in world history. St Ann's Square, in the shadow of St Ann's Church, has recaptured a fleeting semblance of Acresfield, the busy market it once was. The area is now pedestrian, with a large fountain in the middle, and surrounded by shops. At Christmas time stalls are set out selling individual handmade crafts and hot mulled wine, and there is live music and street performers. A reminder of the passing of history is served by the statue of two soldiers, one fallen, with rifles, looking out from the square towards the cathedral, which is a memorial to the men of the Manchester Regiment who gave their lives in the Boer War (1899–1902). Manchester is finding an identity of its own again. Hoardings around the recently re-laid Piccadilly Gardens proclaim 'this is not Paris/Florence/Amsterdam/Washington/... etc... this is Manchester'.

To quote David Lloyd George in 1939: 'Manchester... has a stout heart, an independent heart, unbroken... I am proud of it.'

Glynis Cooper 2002

Ancoats

The name Ancoats first appears in 1212 as Elnecot, derived from the old English *ana cots* which means 'lonely cottages'. This romantic image of Ancoats is almost impossible to imagine at the dawn of the 21st century, but until the advent of the Industrial Revolution, which turned Ancoats into the first industrial suburb in the world, it was simply one of a number of small townships (or villages) which surrounded Manchester. To give some idea of scale, a survey of 1773 reveals that there were then some 30 of these townships, with a total population of 1,905 living in 311 houses. Just 25 years later the first mills were built and the face of Ancoats changed forever.

Ancoats is bounded by Oldham Street, Great Ancoats Street, the Ashton Canal and Pollard Street. Murray Mill, built in 1798, was an early steam-driven mill and one of the first mills to be built in Ancoats. At first, like their neighbours, McConnell and Kennedy, Adam and George Murray were spinning machine makers, before deciding to use their machines themselves for spinning. As the cotton industry grew the Murray brothers extended their first mill (which became known as the Old Mill), adding Decker Mill in 1801, followed by New Mill on Jersey Street in 1804. The three mills were then joined by a series of smaller buildings to form a courtyard which was entered by a 'Great Gate'. Within the courtyard a canal basin was built and linked by a tunnel to the Rochdale Canal. This complex still exists and is part of a proposed urban regeneration programme.

Other early Ancoats mills included Jersey Mill and the Beehive Mill, both on Jersey Street, and the picturesquely named Pin Mill on Pin Mill Brow. Towards the end of the 19th century, Murrays

North West Gas Board Works, Bradford Road, in 1963. The unusually ornate clock tower and entrance way display pride in the industry.

Pollard's Cotton Twist Mill on Great Ancoats Street in 1825.

amalgamated with McConnell and Kennedy to become Manchester Fine Spinners. The new company built more mills: Little Mill in 1908, Paragon Mill and Royal Mill in 1912. Royal Mill stood on the site of McConnell and Kennedy's first steam-driven mill, built in 1794, which was demolished to make way for the new building. The British textile industry started to decline during the 1930s however; a decline which became terminal in the 1960s as a result of cheap cotton imports from the East.

Late 19th-century tenements. Jersey dwellings in 1893.

Hatting was associated with the textile industry, and while Ancoats was not a principal hatting area it was home to the last hatblock manufacturing business in Britain. William Plant and Son tucked themselves away in 'the place', as their works became known, an old three-storey building behind the façade of Great Ancoats Street. The firm finally closed down in 1972; but the machinery and the skilfully crafted hatblocks on which hats were fashioned (including military models for both World Wars and one for a single hat made for the Queen of Tonga to attend the coronation of Queen Elizabeth II) are now preserved in the Hatting Museum at Stockport.

Ancoats has been immortalised by Howard Spring in his novels *Fame is the Spur* and *My Son, My Son*, and in *The Manchester Man* by Mrs Linnaeus Banks. One of the earliest free libraries was opened in Ancoats in 1857. Some education for children was provided 50 years before it became compulsory to do so. Baird Street School (built in 1825) was later amalgamated with St Andrew's School (built 1836). There was a Ragged School in Heyrod Street around 1844 and a school on Major Street. In 1876 a Board School was built on George Leigh Street and to save space a playground was built on the flat roof. The school is still in use today.

Fête Day at the Methodist Church Victoria Hall in 1893.

St Peter's Church was built on Jersey Street in 1859 but fell into disuse after a century of worship. It is now in the process of being restored. St Paul's Church across Oldham Road was not so fortunate and was demolished during the 1960s. St Andrew's Church, built in 1829 on Travis Street, survived until 1961. During demolition four coffins were found

Mills and workers housing in close proximity. Potts Street 1898.

sealed in a secret tomb beneath the altar. The congregation of nearby St Clement's Church in Baird Street, which has not survived either, came from 'a rough and densely peopled part of Ancoats parish' which was deemed to be 'the oldest and worst working district of Manchester'.

The cramped two-up two-down housing of the workers, the back-to-backs (some of which still remain in Portugal Street) and the Victorian courts and tenements (like those of Victoria Square), so graphically described by Engels in *Conditions of the Working Class in England* (1844), differ almost unbelievably from a description of Ancoats as remembered by an old man in 1874; an Ancoats which is unrecognisable in the present day. He recalled '...a pleasing view of another Manchester seat... (that of) the Mosleys, Ancoats Old Hall. On the site of Every Street... stood Love Lane with its ivy mantled cottages and green hedgerows... the lane commanded a sweet variety of scenes to the south-east; fertile valleys and meadows...'

The Round House , built as a circular Swedenborgian church, which became an annexe of Manchester University in the 1930s, and a community centre during the 1940s.

Ancoats Old Hall, a moated grange, was a delightful black and white timbered structure which stood on the corner of

Ancoats Hall (which became part of Manchester Art Museum) on Every Street, in 1900. It was known as the Horsfall Museum and was reported to have haunted vaults.

Every Street. Like most old manor houses of a certain age in this area there is a legend that Bonnie Prince Charlie spent some time there during his march south in 1745 to claim the English crown. Sadly the hall was demolished by George Murray in 1829.

During the 1860s the Midland Railway built a goods depot in Ancoats and a branch line to connect with the main line of the Manchester, Sheffield and Lincolnshire railway at Ashburys. A truncated bridge on this line can still be seen near Ardwick station. The construction of the railway necessitated the demolition of a considerable number of houses and the population of Ancoats decreased by 3,000. Also demolished was Ancoats Independent Chapel, a triangular building which stood on the corner of Great Ancoats Street and Palmerston Street. The line was completed in 1870 and remained in use for just over a century.

The Ancoats population is cosmopolitan and includes Irish, Polish and Italian communities. Irish navvies helped to build railways, reservoirs, roads and canals in the 19th century and their descendants have remained in the area. There is an Irish festival held each year in Manchester. Polish refugees from war-torn Europe flocked to the area to find work in the mills and formed their own prominent groups and societies. According to early directories, Italians have been resident in Ancoats since before 1800. Close to New Cross in Ancoats was an area known as Little Italy.

The Italian workers brought their own skills, which included the making of delicious ice-cream. In April 1811 the *Manchester Chronicle* reported the opening of an ice room at Mary Jozeph's Fruit and Italian Warehouse. As the textile industry declined, enterprising Italian ice-cream manufacturers rented units in disused cotton mills for making and refrigerating their wares. There was a large ice works in Blossom Street and the ice-cream industry prospered within the Italian community.

In Ancoats the wheel of the industrial revolution has turned full circle. Some of the mills are now Grade II listed buildings to be preserved as part of the national heritage and some have been utilised as music performance studios and nightclubs. There are several regeneration projects in progress to improve housing and amenities in the area. The population is small today, maybe only a couple of thousand, but the aim is to transform the world's first industrial suburb into the world's first urban village.

Further reading:
Sutton, Les *Mainly around Ardwick* 3 vols, Manchester 1975, 1977, 1981
Williams, Mike *The mills of Ancoats* Manchester, 1993.
O'Rourke, Aidan *Ancoats – first industrial suburb in the world* Eyewitness Series, 2000 at www.manchesteronline.co.uk/ewm
Di Felice, Serafino *Italians in Ancoats* Virtual Manchester, 2001 at www.manchester.com/nojava/localnews/community/italians/ancoats

Ardwick

Ardwick takes its name from the Saxon king Aethelred, Ard being considered a shortened form of the name. *Wic* is an old English word for a farm, dwelling or village. A survey of 1320 records mills, fisheries and ovens. Tenants of Ardwick were to grind their corn at the 'Mill of Mamcestre' and to use the bakehouse at Lords Court. An annual license to fish for trout in the River Medlock cost one shilling. There are limestone beds under and around the Medlock and a sketch of Ardwick in 1841 revealed that fossil fish had been found there. It is most likely that Ardwick began life as Aethelred's farm and grew into a village. It was certainly a village by Tudor times and rather a lively one judging by the records of the Court Leet, the magistrates court of its day. There were problems with wild women, disorderly houses, children playing 'giddy-gaddy' (cat's pallet), footballs breaking windows, and the number of dunghills on the roads.

However, by the time of the Industrial Revolution, at least part of Ardwick had gone upmarket. In 1830 Ardwick Green was described as 'a pleasant approach to Manchester, being well planted and ornamented with elegant houses on the border of a canal...' It was an area of pleasant and fashionable houses, rather more countrified than some of its neighbours; a popular neighbourhood favoured by merchants. One such merchant was Mr John Potter. In 1787 his land covered the area from Viaduct Street to the scrub land on the north side of the present day Ardwick railway station. His third son, James, also a merchant, married a girl from Lancaster's mayoral family. James Potter's son, Edmund, was born in the family home and became

St Thomas's Church in 1900. The house on the left (31 Ardwick Green, built 1741) was the mansion in The Manchester Man *by Mrs Linnaeus Banks.*

Nicholls Hospital (later the Ellen Wilkinson School), Hyde Road, 1906. Ellen Wilkinson was Minister of Education during the late 1940s.

the grandfather of the internationally acclaimed children's writer, Beatrix Potter.

Ardwick stretches from the River Medlock in the north to the other side of the Cornbrook in the south. Higher Ardwick is the area towards Ashton Old Road, which as late as 1890 still contained the nostalgically named Donkey Common, where travelling circuses would perform. Ardwick Green centres on the modern busy roundabout where Stockport Road (the A6) and Hyde Road (the A57) meet. The first mill was built in 1800 on Union Street. Ardwick Limeworks lay near the Medlock, close to Ashton Old Road, along with the Ardwick Iron Works, the Spindle Works and a brickworks. Rubber works and dye works stood by the Medlock while there were sawmills and boilerworks, chemical works and brickworks in the southern part of the township. Discharge from the chemical works and brickworks, along with other effluent, polluted the Cornbrook so much that it became known as the Black Brook. Streets of dark cramped houses were built, often by those who knew little about construction, where increasing numbers of workers lived in the squalid conditions which so horrified Engels in 1844.

In 1840 the first section of the Manchester and Birmingham Railway opened, which ran across Ardwick, effectively separating Higher Ardwick from what became known as Lower Ardwick. Eight years later the 'Ardwick Extension Railway' opened 'uniting the Lancashire and Yorkshire Railway on the north side with the London and North Western and Manchester, Sheffield and Lincolnshire Railway in the south.' The latter ran across what had formerly been Mr John Potter's land. The line had two remarkable viaducts: the first crossing the River Medlock and the Ashton Canal by means of a single 100ft span with four supporting arches of a 30ft span each; the second being 770 yards in length, which stretched from some distance north of Ashton

Old Road to Chancery Lane. There were also subsidiary lines, which have not survived, from Ardwick to Ancoats goods depot and to Miles Platting. The Ardwick and Ancoats Dispensary, which had opened in 1828 on Ancoats Lane, was displaced by the Midland Railway during the late 1860s and moved to Mill Street before being superseded by the opening of Ancoats Hospital in 1874.

Mannings Toy Shop on Ashton Old Road in 1909.

Close to Hyde Road stood Ardwick Hall, home in turn to two of Ardwick's most influential families: the Birches, a military family of the 17th and 18th centuries, and the Mosleys of the 19th century, who were rubber manufacturers, making mackintoshes and waterproofs. The hall stood, surrounded by gardens, in Summer Place (now Devonshire Street) on land presently occupied by Great Universal Stores. Ardwick Cemetery, where John Dalton (who, in 1810, was the first to put forward atomic theory) is buried, lies alongside Devonshire Street on the west side. Adjacent to the cemetery and fronting on to Hyde Road, Nicholls Hospital, a boys school modelled on Chetham's College, was built in 1881 by Alderman Benjamin Nicholls (who owned a mill on Chapel Street and was twice mayor of Manchester) as a memorial to his only son. The school later became known as the Ellen Wilkinson School. Ellen Wilkinson was born in Coral Street in Ardwick. She became an MP in 1924 and took part in the Jarrow hunger march of 1936, becoming Minister for Education in the post-World War Two government of Clement Attlee.

There were 29 day schools in Ardwick in 1834 though they catered for less than half the child population of the area. The first Ragged School in Manchester (for poor and deprived children) was opened in around 1852 in Dark Lane by Edward Gibbs, a professor of music. He taught his pupils hymns and gave them hot drinks and soup. It later became part of St Gregory's RC School. There were several churches in Ardwick with schools attached, such as St Silas's Church, St Aloysius's Church in Ogden Street, the United Methodist Chapel on Hyde Road, and there was a truants school on Mill Street. Ross Place School, near Stockport Road, established a claim to fame in the 20th century by having on its pupil roll Harry H. Corbett, co-star of the well-known BBC comedy series *Steptoe and Son*.

On the corner of Hyde Road and Devonshire Street (opposite the Ellen Wilkinson School) the tram depot built in 1903 still stands. It was used by Manchester Corporation Trams and North Western Buses (among others) and today it is the main Manchester depot for Stagecoach. During the last hundred years the depot has witnessed the transition from horse-drawn trams and omnibuses to the sleek modern 'lo-liners' of the 21st century. About half a mile further east along Hyde Road the Fenian Arch stood at New Bank Street. Demolished during the 1970s, it was a memorial to the 'Manchester Martyrs', three Irishmen executed in 1867 for assisting the escape from custody of two Fenian leaders during which a police sergeant was shot dead.

Ardwick Green, 1921. This was a merchants' residential area in the 18th and 19th centuries. Note the street cobbles known as 'petrified kidneys'.

Ardwick Green was the hub of Victorian Ardwick. The pond on the green featured in *The Manchester Man* by Mrs Linnaeus Banks, who lived in Ardwick Green for a while; as did John Rylands who founded

The Apollo Cinema at the corner of Hyde Road/Stockport Road in 1950. It is now used mainly for rock concerts.

the university library. St Thomas's Church stands on Ardwick Green North. The church was built in 1741 on a site given by the Birch family, many of whom lie within its grounds. It is one of the oldest Manchester churches still standing. In 1751 the Birches endowed St Thomas's School, which was built adjoining the church. One of the residents of Ardwick Green at this time was Robert Peel, grandfather of Sir Robert Peel who was responsible for the foundation of the modern police force and the abolition of the corn laws. Ardwick Town Hall stood on Ardwick Green North near the quaintly named Polygon, full of trees and gracious pleasant houses, now built up with shops and modern housing. There were also three breweries in the vicinity, in Chapel Street, Brodie Street and Downing Street; but the houses in these areas were dirty and damp, condemned as some of the worst in Manchester.

Emmanuel Baptist Church in 1965. Workers' cottages have been converted to house the church.

Heywood House on Bennett Street in 1972. Modern flats replaced the old back-to-backs.

built in 1938. Other theatres and cinemas in Ardwick included the Lido Dance Hall in Claribel Street, the Queens Picture House, with Eastern scenes painted on its walls, the Roy Cinema and the Metropole Theatre on Ashton Old Road, and the Princes Picture House in Grey Mare Lane. Pubs in the localities, such as the Apsley, the Shakespeare, the Ivy Bower and the Union did a roaring trade with cinema and theatre patrons.

Ardwick has had a chequered history; especially since the Industrial Revolution. Although there is no specific regeneration plan for Ardwick, which currently has a population of around 10,700, new estates of smart red-brick houses have been built in the area around Ardwick station and there is a development plan to revitalise much of East Manchester. This includes the building of a brand-new stadium for the Commonwealth Games in 2002. The stadium lies on Ashton New Road near the boundaries of Ardwick with Clayton and Miles Platting. Other sporting facilities, such as an Olympic-size swimming pool, are also being built close by. So the future for Ardwick may lie in the world of sport, while the mills and factories, the blackened streets of damp little houses and the former elegance of Ardwick Green will fade into a folk memory.

Ardwick Barracks stood on Ardwick Green North. The Barracks (known as the Drill Hall) were officially opened in 1887, the home of the 1st Manchester Volunteer Battalion formed in 1859 by an amalgamation of the 28th and 33rd Lancashire Rifle Volunteers. In 1889 their name was changed to the 5th (Ardwick) Volunteer Battalion; and again in 1908, when the Territorial Army was formed, to the 8th (Ardwick) Battalion. In 1892 a five-storey building with a 90ft tower was constructed adjoining the Drill Hall to house the works of Jewsbury and Brown, celebrated manufacturers of 'aerated mineral waters and ginger beer'. However, the company manufactured 'oriental toothpaste' as well. It is not recorded how this differs from the brands available on chemist's shelves today.

The southern part of Ardwick Green was the entertainment centre of Ardwick. There was the Ardwick Empire Theatre (later the New Manchester Hippodrome Theatre); the Coliseum; the Ardwick Picture Theatre (formerly the Victoria Picture Palace); a billiard hall behind the Empire and a wrestling stadium behind the picture theatre. Travelling fairs would stop on the common land on the corner of Brunswick Street, which lay opposite the theatres. All that survives today is the Apollo,

Further reading:

Sutton, Les *Mainly about Ardwick* 3 vols, Manchester, 1975, 1977, 1981.

Makepeace, Chris *Looking back at Hulme, Moss Side, Chorlton on Medlock and Ardwick* Willow Publishing, 1995.

Beswick

Beswick first emerges from the historical records as *Beaces hlaw* in 917. *Hlaw* is an Anglo-Saxon word for a natural hill used as a burial mound. Later, in around 1200, the name was altered to *Beaces wic* (Anglo-Saxon for farm). All that can be said with any certainty is that Beswick has its origins in the Anglo-Saxon period, but any hard evidence will be buried deep beneath the foundations of the Industrial Revolution. It was very much a part of the millscapes. Beswick's identity has been subsumed in recent times and today it is bracketed with Clayton in terms of politics and population. Not one of the larger suburbs, it lies on the east side of Manchester and is centred mainly around Ashton Old and New Roads and Grey Mare Lane. Today Grey Mare Lane has an open-air market, a Queen Vic pub, and blocks of concrete flats, while Ashton Old Road is still full of Victorian terrace houses built for the workers in the mills.

It is difficult to trace a separate history for Beswick, but glimpses are revealed through odd sentences in the history of other suburbs. Thus it is learned that St Mary's was the parish church of Beswick; that St Brigid's was the local Catholic church with its own primary school; that there were schools on Nansen Street, Birley Street and Hillkirk Street; that Beswick Co-operative Society was founded in June 1892 with a membership of just seven men and had its headquarters on Rowsley Street; that the CWS bakeries were based in Beswick; that the local cinemas were the Don, the Mosley and the New Royal; that Whit Walks still took place as late as the 1960s; and that there were glue works, starch works and breweries in the area as well as the textile mills.

Sandown Street in 1903, showing the drabness of living in close proximity to the works and chimney on Hillkirk Street.

Ashton New Road in 1902 before the road was widened. Lack of traffic makes it almost unrecognisable.

CWS Bakeries, 1962.

Beswick was incorporated with Manchester in 1838 in the original borough. Council minutes from 1851 reveal that the state of the roads, footpaths and street lights in Beswick was giving cause for concern. Beswick inhabitants questioned their financial liability for providing for these services. For a while there was an impasse before a lamplighter and cleaner was appointed so that 'if the road was in a bad state at least it was lit, and, in spite of the customary reluctance of the inhabitants to pay for improvements, some start had been made to put Beswick on the map.' A century and half later little has changed!

The most delightful snippets however, are to be found through the local newspapers of the day. A big annual event in Beswick was Silcocks Fair, which was held on Hillkirk Street croft shortly before Christmas. An account of the fair by two small boys in the early decades of the 20th century has survived and their excitement fairly crackles from the pages. They describe the popular tunes played by huge fairground organs; the steamboats; flea circus; the roll-penny boards, sideshows and boxing booths; the rides; and 'everywhere, screaming, shouting, rumbling, roaring, cracking of air rifles, and shrieking of klaxon as a successful hit raises the skeleton from his coffin…' The boys finally decide to go on the Animal Ride 'its organ thumping out in quick jerky tempo *Always in All Ways*, the smiling metal marionettes beating time as the animals race round, simultaneously bobbing up and down in a crazy circuit…'

They choose long-necked metal giraffes and 'are soon accelerated into a frenzied, bucking, torso jerking vertigo'. What really fascinates them however, is the Freak Show. There is the 'largest rat in the world, trapped in a Liverpool sewer after maiming its captor'. They ask for details of the maiming in typical small boy fashion but their curiosity remains unsatisfied. The two-headed chicken leaves them distinctly unimpressed and they are disappointed with the Petrified Miner, having 'expected something finer than the slumped tatty anthropoid that leered at us from the large cardboard box.' Today such innocent excitement at the travelling fairs is something which has long since disappeared.

There are also descriptions of markets in 1920s and 1930s Beswick. The sloping Dr Buck's Croft had flare-lit stalls, and free samples were offered by the toffee-makers stalls, but the largest crowds always gathered around the floor coverings, whose sellers 'slapped and eulogised the rolls of cheap oilcloth as though they were selling Axminster'. Many houses at the time had 'paved living rooms',

Ashton New Road on 20 February 1936.

which meant that floors were damp and uneven and no floor covering lasted long. Grey Mare Lane Market was full of open stalls, then as now, where home-made pies and puddings, cakes and crumpets for teatime could be purchased to eat in front of a glowing coal fire. Shopping was done on a daily basis before the days of fridges and freezers but on Saturdays children would accompany their mothers in the hope of a small treat like a stick of liquorice or a toffee apple.

As the textile industry slowly failed in the years following World War Two, areas like Beswick declined and wide-scale clearances were undertaken, adding to the depressed feel and appearance of the place. High-rise deck-access blocks of flats like Fort Beswick on Bell Crescent were built, but within a few years were suffering the effects of poor workmanship, vermin infestation and vandalism. In 1975 Manchester Housing Committee admitted to 'making a big mistake' with these blocks of flats. As with the 'Hulme Crescents' the high-rise blocks also destroyed local community life.

Beswick ended the 20th century on a low note, but thanks to the East Manchester Regeneration Scheme business and building are now returning to the area and there is a modern Corporation housing estate on Hinkley Street. The Commonwealth Games are being staged in Manchester in 2002 and a brand-new stadium has been built on the borders of Beswick with Clayton and Miles Platting. This has brought new jobs, new housing and a new sense of self-respect to Beswick and the future now looks brighter for this small suburb than it has done for many years.

Further reading:
Sutton, Les *Mainly about Ardwick* 3 vols, Manchester, 1975, 1977, 1981
Beswick with Clayton ward profile 1991 Manchester City Council, 1993

Buffalo Bill Cody (on tram platform) with genuine real-life Indian chiefs and braves on a visit to the UK in 1903.

Blackley

Blackley, the 'clearing in a dark wood', lies on the northern edge of Manchester. Mediaeval Blackley, like Moston, was part of the demesne belonging to the lord of the manor of Manchester. The area was covered with thick deciduous woodlands of oak, ash and elm. The woods were full of fallow deer and a number of wolves, an occupational hazard of hunting

McKenna's Brewery on the aptly named Brewery Street in 1885.

at the time. A survey of 1322 deemed these woodlands to be worth 53s 10d (about £825 today) in terms of pannage (fruits of the forest, honey produced, etc) and £133 6s 8d (just over £42,000) in terms of timber. Timber could only be cut and deer could only be hunted on payment of dues (assarts) to the king. Otherwise the serf had to make do with wolf or rabbit for his cooking pot. The River Irk, which flows through Boggart Hole/ Blackley Clough, was famed for its eels, highly regarded in the England of the Middle Ages, although they are not to modern tastes for the most part.

Blackley Hall, which lay on Valentine's Brow close to the junction with Rochdale Road and Middleton Road, was built in Tudor times by the Assheton family mentioned in William Harrison Ainsworth's *Lancashire Witches*. The hall was a fine half-timbered building typical of the architecture of the time, according to Booker in 1857, although it did not

Pikes Fold Cottages, 1888.

survive beyond 1815. The hall was bought by the Legh family of Lyme Hall (Disley) in 1636 and then let and sublet. Mrs Shay, the wife of one of the tenants, was said to haunt the hall because she was alleged not to have died a natural death, but to have been murdered within the hall. She was supposed to have been accompanied by a little black dog rather reminiscent of the Black Shuck stories of East Anglia. Whatever the truth of the matter, the hall gained a reputation and it was sold in 1815 for a ridiculously low price and demolished. A printworks was built on the site but it failed to prosper and local people spoke of the curse of Old Shay's wife.

The Byron family leased the Blackley estate from the de la Warre family (lords of Manchester) during the 1400s. The Byrons built a small oratory or

Boggart Hole Clough, once haunted by a boggart or mischievous spirit. Kay's Farm in 1890.

United Methodist Free Church mission van with its message of doom, 12 March 1892.

chapel in Blackley, which was recorded by John Leland in his *Itinerary* of 1538. In later centuries this chapel became the Episcopal Chapel and Church of St Peter in Blackley. The church was rebuilt in 1736 and then again in 1844 on a site adjacent to that on which the original chapel had been built in the 15th century. The romantic and colourful 19th-century poet, Lord Byron, was a descendant of this family.

Blackley escaped the worst excesses of the Industrial Revolution and remained a pretty rural farming area until the turn of the 20th century. There were lush meadows surrounded by hawthorn hedges around the River Irk. A water-driven corn mill, shown on 18th-century maps as a working mill, used to stand on the river bank near Hollow Lane. The remains of the weir for the mill can still be seen. Heaton Mills were built close by for the dyeing and printing of textiles. Linen weaving had been a cottage industry since the 16th century when French immigrants, escaping religious persecution in their own country, settled in the north of England, bringing their crafts with them.

French Barn Lane, 1895.

Oakworth Street in 1898.

Middleton Road was turnpiked in the 18th century and there was a toll house on the Middleton-Prestwich boundary. There was also an old smithy on the Middleton Road, near to the entrance to Heaton Park.

An aerial view of Booth Hall children's hospital in 1925.

Heaton Park was built by the Egerton family in 1772. The designer was James Wyatt, an architect of some renown. Some of his interior work was inspired by Robert Adam. Guests as diverse as the Duke of Wellington and the actress, Fanny Kemble, stayed at Heaton Hall when visiting Manchester. Heaton Park, the grounds in which the hall stands, covers 640 acres, making it Manchester's largest park. The park contains a large boating lake, fronted by the façade of Manchester's first Town Hall, which was in King Street and was demolished in 1912. It is described as 'an architectural copy of the Greek Erechtheion in Athens'. Today the park has 'swan boats' on the boating lake, a huge rock set in a field which is known as the Papal Monument, and a tram museum. Old tram tracks are still visible in the park. The Orangery at the Hall has been transformed into a restaurant and conference centre, and a farm centre has been established where Highland cattle, the little black-faced Soay sheep, peacocks and waterfowl are bred.

Boggart Hole Clough, near the hall, was haunted in its prettier, more peaceful days by a boggart. One story tells of a farm at the head of the Clough near White Moss. The farmer and his family of several children were plagued by a boggart, 'an unquiet spirit that manifested itself in a small shrill voice like a baby's penny trumpet...' At first the boggart was fairly harmless until one of the sons of the house poked fun at it. The boggart took great exception to this and things started to get a bit heavy with some injuries being inflicted. Finally the boggart tried to suffocate one of the farmer's children in bed. The

Foxholes, 1935.

Children's Hospital stands opposite, but this particular boggart does not seem to have cared much for the march of progress and it is many years now since it was either seen or heard.

Heaton Park was used during World War One for billeting and training soldiers near Hollows Lane and there was a mock-up of the infamous battlefield trenches of France. This now lies under a pitch and putt golf course. There was also a hospital in a large house at the top of Bowker Vale in World War One. During this period a musician with a hurdy-gurdy or a barrel organ (both of which he hired in Ancoats) would come and play at the bottom of Hollows Lane on summer evenings. Where Hollows Lane crossed Victoria Avenue at the top end was known as 'Top o' the arbor' or 'Top o' t' windy arbor' before being renamed Heaton Park Road. St Peter's Mission Church and School lay at the junction of Heaton Park Road (now Weardale Road), Crab Lane and Munn Lane (now Ryther Grove). Crab Lane had a school, a post office, a Methodist chapel, and 'the

farmer had had enough. He packed up his family and moved to new premises.

A later legend, however, paints a kinder picture of the boggart. 'Tread softly,' wrote the story teller, 'for this Boggart Clough, and see in yonder dark corners, and beneath projecting mossy stones, where the dusky sullen cave yawns before you... there lurks a strange elf, the sly and mischievous boggart...' Young men would try to win the love of a particular girl by 'going into the Clough for three grains of St John's fernseed in which the boggart frolicked...'

The Clough is still wooded and today Booth Hall

The ICI works (dyestuffs division) in the late 1950s.

Heaton Hall in 1902.

tallest hencote in Lancashire' which was a single mill chimney that had once been part of a dye works. Blackley was 'too far out for the cotton mills', but, like Harpurhey, played a part in the dyeing and bleaching side of the textile industry. Close to Crab Lane and St Andrews Church lay a row of cottages known as Boggart Hole Cottages, which were demolished to make way for Blackley cemetery.

Blackley remained reasonably rural until the 1930s, although it had been incorporated with Manchester in 1890. There was haymaking and the gathering of root crops such as swedes, turnips and mangel wurzels. Corncrakes, now quite rare, could be heard in the meadows. Several farms had survived, among them Clarksons Farm, Acre Top Farm, Munn Lane Farm and New Bridge Farm on Hollows Lane, and there were cottages along the riverside. The 1930s was known as 'the building era'. This can best be illustrated by the following anecdote. New Bridge Farm was sold in 1935. A year later the farm had been demolished and the land covered with houses. Plane Trees Cottages went the same way. Now the population stands at about 11,500, a 4 percent decline on 1991, but still far more than the peaceful village of a century before.

The smithy on Middleton Road near the entrance to Heaton Park, 6 August 1901.

Today Blackley is a very different place. Echoes of the past can be seen in some of the place names like the Meadows School, Plant Hill Adult Education Centre and French Barn Lane. More schools and churches, such as St Clare's Church and primary school, Victoria Avenue Community Primary School and Blackley Pentecostal Church have been built. There are high-rise blocks of flats in Crab Village and Corporation housing on Victoria Avenue. A Jewish cemetery is laid out along Rochdale Road and there is a synagogue on nearby Middleton Road. An industrial area lies around Blackley New Road (Avecia is one of the larger companies operating there). There are a lot of boarded up terraced houses and there is a lot of property for sale. In one or two areas there is an air of shabby gentility. The local library looks as though it has been fortified. If the boggart of Boggart Hole Clough genuinely has left town, it is, in some respects, not difficult to understand why.

Further reading:

Jackson, C.S. *Down Hollow Lane* Neil Richardson, 1990
McGill, Hilda M. *History of Blackley* Blackley Library, 1939

Bradford

While Bradford in Yorkshire is a well-known town, there are those who have taken some persuading that there is a Bradford in Manchester as well. Bradford is actually the name of a bona fide suburb of Manchester, which is bordered by Miles Platting, Clayton and the other side of Ashton New Road from Beswick. Bradford is first mentioned in 1119 as 'Broad Ford'. This may refer to a crossing place, now lost, of the River Medlock. Bradford in mediaeval times was good pasture land and there would have been water meadows around the Medlock. There were also woodlands full of roe deer and wild bees, which produced sufficient honey for marketable consumption. Hawk, heron and eagles nested in the woodlands and there would have been wolves roaming around until at least 1400.

Little is known of these centuries of halcyon rural bliss which Bradford must have enjoyed. The suburb's proximity to Manchester and the river sealed its fate when the Industrial Revolution arrived. Bradford also had another commodity which made it attractive to industry. The mills and manufactories and, later, the trains used for transport, needed coal. Bradford had a colliery close to the city centre, and after incorporation with the city in 1885, within the Manchester municipal boundaries. There were other pits, such as those at Oldham, Ashton, Hyde, Denton and Dukinfield, but the roads were bad and the canals were slow. Bradford was close to the city centre and to the millscapes of Ancoats, Ardwick, Beswick, Chorlton on Medlock, Hulme and Miles Platting. Coal of course was also required for fuel by the rapidly increasing population. Bradford Colliery began

Mill Street, showing the Ashton Canal running along the back of the mills, 1897.

The Wellington Inn on Ashton Old Road, 1970. Bradford Colliery is in the background.

production during the 1790s. It was active for nearly 200 years and, like all pits, suffered the occasional accident but none that rated as a disaster. To the thousands of exhausted textile workers straggling home was added a sight more familiar to the Welsh valleys, that of miners with their coal-blackened faces and their hobnail boots clacking against the cobbles. Bradford pithead machinery loomed large on the Manchester millscapes and became a familiar landmark until it was demolished in 1973.

Bradford also had another distinction; that of having one of the first two public parks in Manchester. Philips Park opened in 1846. The park was named after Mark Philips, who was one of the first two MPs for the borough of Manchester after the Reform Act of 1832 had been passed. He had recognised that the workers needed somewhere pleasant to spend their Sunday afternoons now that 'we all have increased leisure time' (as local mill-owner, Edmund Potter, grandfather of Beatrix Potter, had put it). Mark Philips was a benevolent and charitable man and the establishment of public parks was one of his particular enthusiasms. He was also responsible for Queens Park in Harpurhey which opened the same year.

Philips Park covered 30 acres and had colourful flower beds, a lake, glasshouses and a number of walks; a reminiscent glimpse for many of the countryside which they had so recently lost. However, not everyone appeared to enjoy walking in the park on Sundays. A rather mournful description from a disenchanted worker has survived. 'Sunday – just a passing of darkness and light like any other day but its association with church and so with death renders it faintly oppressive. This is felt particularly at Philips Park with its great cemetery on the other side of the Medlock...'

Perhaps the writer who wasn't too keen on Philips Park would have preferred the 'Simmies Shows' for entertainment. The shows, performed by John Simpson and his wife, Elizabeth, and their children, were played on Mill Street in Bradford and at Holt Town, and sometimes in Ardwick during the last years of the 19th century. John Simpson and his son, Enoch, always played the bad guys, while Sally Simpson, Enoch's wife, gave displays on horseback. Some of their performances were a little ambitious, to say the least, and included *Hannibal's Crossing of the Alps* and *Ali Baba and the Forty Thieves*. During one production a particular scene called for a moving light, which was effected by a man holding a lantern. His cue for the light was 'Aha! I see a light!' One evening he tripped and accidentally set the backdrop curtains on fire which led to a slight amendment of the script. 'Aha! I see a light! The bloody show's on fire!'

Cooling towers at Stuart Street Power Station in August 1973.

Knocker-up, 1943. Early morning call in the days before alarm clocks.

In 1869 Bradford Gas Works was built on the corner of Bradford Road and Hulme Hall Lane, close to the Ashton Canal and the Lancashire and Yorkshire Railway. The works began manufacturing gas in 1884. However, the works were near the cemetery and Philips Park. This caused a lot of controversy, exacerbated by one councillor saying that 'a whiff of gas would improve rather than spoil the amenities of Philips Park'. The gas holder was 259ft (over 83m) high and must have seemed very intrusive and overwhelming. During the prolonged and freezing winter of 1946–47 local inhabitants queued up for coke from the gas works to stoke up their open fires and keep themselves warm.

St Brigid's Church and the Presbyterian Church, both on Mill Street, and Christ Church on Carfax Street, looked after the spiritual needs of Bradford. St Brigid's and Christ Church also had schools attached. There were other schools, including the Queen Street Board School and Adsbury Primary School. Much of old Bradford has now, however, disappeared, and many former features are just a memory. These include the lamplighters, whose duties were to light and clean the gas lamps; a bookshop which sold American comics of 'horror, terror, and legendary weird tales'; and the shop on

Beaumont Street, 1910. Coronation celebrations for King George V.

Hawke Street with Bradford Colliery, 1963.

Forge Lane which sold ginger beer and large fruity Eccles cakes.

Today Bradford has a population of around 10,600, a fall of 8 percent from 1991. Like its neighbours, Bradford is part of the East Manchester Regeneration Scheme. The new stadium for the Commonwealth Games 2002 has risen on the borders where Bradford meets Beswick and Clayton. Bradford is now home to a velodrome for the National Cycle Centre. There is still a large industrial area in Pottery Lane and, incongruously, a Mercedes-Benz showroom stands opposite a Corporation housing estate. The gas works have survived and so has Philips Park. Bradford, however, is beginning the 21st century on a positive note. Regeneration, rebuilding and the renewal of a communal focus has been provided by the Commonwealth Games. The hawthorn hedges and the green pastures of yesteryear may have disappeared but there is now something to look forward to once again.

Further reading:
Sutton, Les *Mainly about Ardwick* 3 vols, Manchester, 1975, 1977, 1981
Bradford ward profile 1991 Manchester City Council, 1993

Burnage

Burnage is bounded by Levenshulme to the north, Didsbury to the south, Heaton Norris to the east and Withington to the west. It includes the district of Green End and overlaps Ladybarn. The meaning of Burnage is given as 'brown hedge' in 1322. It is not clear to what this refers but stone walls used to be called hedges and Burnage may have been the name given to some type of wall or boundary. There were 16 different ways of spelling Burnage (this may delight students of etymology or Scrabble players, but there are no prizes) which was originally part of Withington and Heaton Norris. Burnage developed along the old salt route from Cheshire to Manchester and Burnage Lane still follows this line. In 1774 there were only 54 houses and the population was 297. Today the population is just over 13,800 people, which means that it has increased over 46 times during the last 220 years. Burnage, however, became in the 20th century a mainly residential suburb – it was never an industrial suburb.

When Burnage Hall was built by John Watts off Burnage Lane in 1840, the village still only had a population of about 500 and occupation was mainly agricultural. John Watts was one of the sons of J. Watts of the firm S. & J. Watts, which had what was termed 'the grandest warehouse' in Britain on Portland Street. It is now the Britannia Hotel, which continues to sport a fantastic façade of carvings and statuary of fish, classical figures and other maritime subjects, on each of its architecturally different storeys. Burnage Hall has not shared the same good fortune. It was demolished in 1911 to make way for the building of the Burnage Park Estate.

The streets were cobbled; the cobbles being known as 'petrified kidneys'. Water came from roadside wells or springs. There was a 'cottage industry of handloom weaving' in the 'Cotton Shops' (a row of tall cottages on Fog Lane) and by John Watts at Barcicroft Cottage. He later helped to found the firm of S. & J. Watts. There was a dame's school run in a cottage at Green End some time before 1872 and subsequently Burnage Congregational Sunday School was established. Burnage Elementary School was built on the site of a house to which the owner had added a tower to serve as his mausoleum. The

'Garden Village' aspects of Burnage in 1910.

Burnage Lane, 1906.

house was demolished after neighbours protested about the intended use of the tower.

St Mary of the Angels and St Clare Church was built in 1853 on Clare Road and rebuilt in 1879. In 1869 the Convent of the Poor Clares opened on Clare Road, followed by St Mary of the Angels and St Clare School in 1870. The church finally closed in 1957 and the buildings became part of the school. A new church was then built on Elbow Street. While it was being built the congregation used the Grand Cinema on Stockport Road. Afterwards the cinema became an antique dealer's business.

In 1894 George Bernard Shaw wrote 'Burnage... is held to be the prettiest village... near Manchester, still untouched in its cottage existence and rusticity as it is endless in foliage... lingering life and loveliness... all the more acceptable for the progress of growth, devouring space, which is going on all around it.' There was a dole field (with shared strips of land) dating back to 1590 called Barcicroft, and as late as 1904 Tanyard Farm, Dahlia Farm, Hyde Fold Farm and High Farm were still working farms. Around 1900 Cringle Brook flowed across farming land, as far as the junction of Ranford Road and Kempton Road, towards Burnage House and Cringle Hall. In 1929 a bandstand was built in Cringle Fields.

The novelist Frances Hodgson Burnett (of *Little*

Burnage Lane. Thatched cottages in 1929.

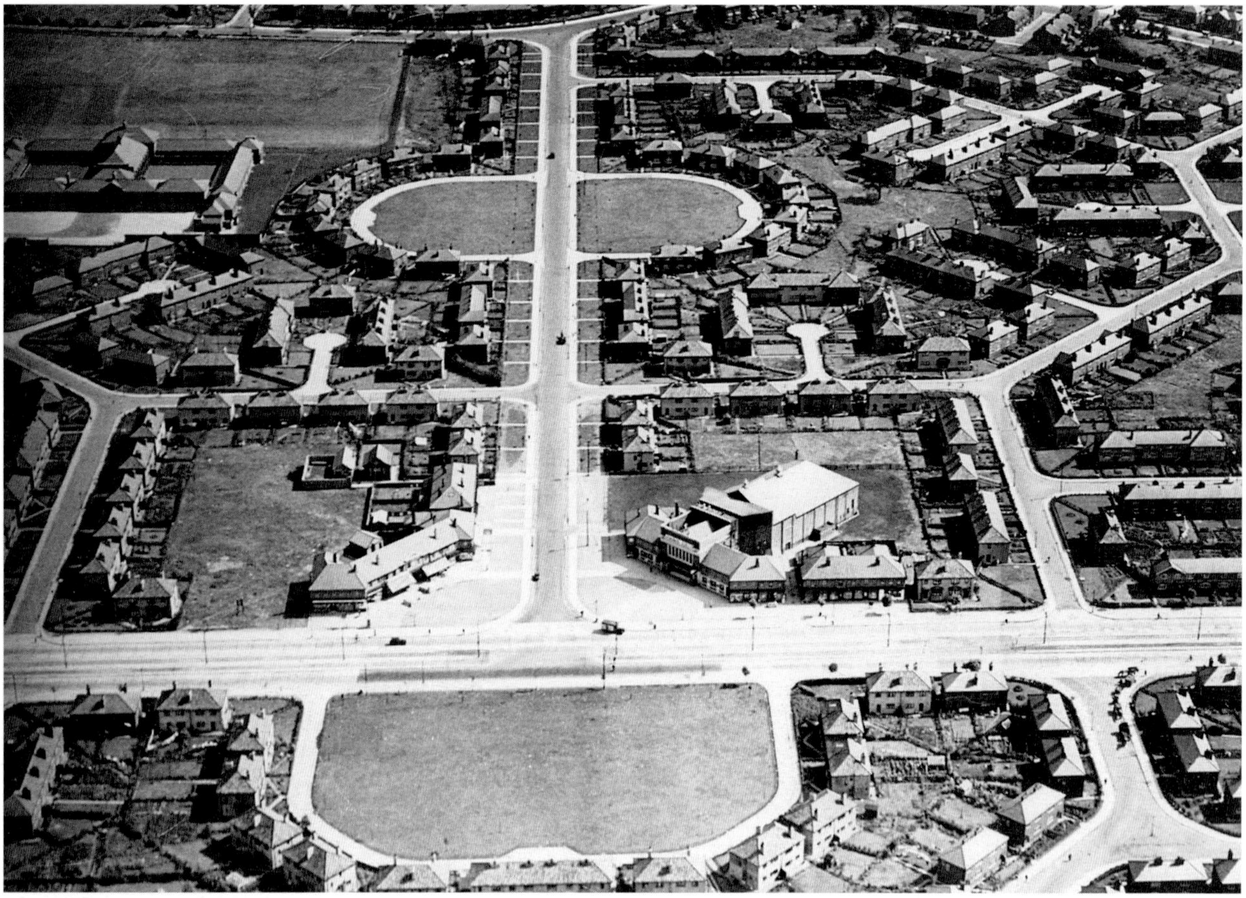

An aerial view of the lido, cinema, Kingsway and Green End Road, 31 August 1932.

Lord Fauntleroy and *The Secret Garden* fame), born in Burnage in 1849, would have had little difficulty in recognising the place.

Change, however, was in the air. In 1906 Manchester Tenants Ltd was formed with the aim of building a pioneering garden suburb to be named Burnage Garden Village. Each tenant held at least two £10 shares and each house was situated 'so as to have the maximum amount of light and air and pleasantness of outlook and also to secure some open space for recreation'. The houses were semi-detached with hot and cold running water, electricity and a bathroom. Local facilities included a bowling green, tennis courts, allotments, a children's playground and a village hall. The village was completed in 1912. In 1911 Grangethorpe Drive was built as a road of 'high class semi-detached villas'. Mauldeth Road led from Green End on Burnage Lane to Mauldeth Hall, which had been the palace of the Bishop of Manchester from 1847–69. Burnage was rapidly becoming a place for people of good breeding to live.

Development continued. Broom Lane and farm workers' cottages in Cradock Fold were demolished. Kingsway was built in 1923, followed by the Kingsway Estate in 1927. The railway had arrived in 1909 and Burnage station was opened on 1 May.

There was also the added attraction of the Burnage Miniature Railway on Moorton Avenue from 1910–30. It was built and run in the garden of Moorton Lodge by Mr T. Foster, close to the High Farm (on Crossley Road) and Dahlia Farm (on Burnage Lane) fields on which the Corporation housing estate would later be built.

A little light industry arrived in the form of Fairey Aviation, Crossley and Hans Renold between the wars. During World War Two Fairey Aviation became a target for German bombers. However, the planes missed the aviation works and succeeded in bombing Burnage High School on Burnage Lane instead on the night of 28 November 1940. The school had only just been built and it needed extensive repair work before re-opening.

Burnage was incorporated with Manchester in

Burnage Lane/Fog Lane, 1900.

1904. Since World War Two there has been steady housing development in the area and it has become a largely residential suburb. Ladybarn, home to St Chad's Church, is the upmarket area, with new show homes built around the centre and Ladybarn Park. Today the population of Burnage and Ladybarn is just under 14,000. A modern claim to fame for Burnage is that it is the home of Liam and Noel Gallagher, brothers, musicians and co-founders of the best-selling rock band Oasis.

Further reading:
Sussex, G., P. Helm and A. Brown *Looking back at Levenshulme and Burnage* Willow Publishing, 1987
http://ds.dial.pipex.com/david.ratcliffe/lhg//vol6/burnage.htm

Cheetham

In 1212, three years before Magna Carta was signed, the name Cheetham first appeared. The name simply means 'the village by the forest or wood'. Cheetham was farming countryside through which ran the 'pleasant stream of the River Irwell'. The village was renowned for its archers, who used to practise on the site on which St Mark's Church was later built. They also practised up on Kersal Moor where the Manchester Races were held during Whit Week. In the mid-1730s, Dick Turpin, the notorious highwayman, was reported in the local papers as a frequent visitor to the races and would doubtless have ridden through Cheetham on his way to Kersal Moor.

The Great Synagogue on Cheetham Hill Road, 1959.

After the road was turnpiked in the 18th century, there was a toll gate at White Smithy Bar, at the junction of Bury Old Road and Middleton Road that is now the site of Halfway House (near the Methodist Church), which used to have fountains for both dogs and horses. There was also the Temple Toll Bar near Smedley Lane. Cheetham Hill Road, formerly York Street, was built in 1820. Cheetham and Cheetham Hill village used to be separate entities but they have now merged into one. Cheetham is the name of the political ward of the city council, though the area is known locally as Cheetham Hill. The township of Cheetham extends to Crescent Road bordering on Crumpsall and includes the village of Cheetham Hill. Boundary Street separates Cheetham from Broughton, which is part of Salford.

Cheetham did not have its own hall as such but it had some fine large houses, including Greenhill, home of banker Samuel Jones; Stocks House, owned by the Ryding family, on the corner of Cheetham Hill Road and North Road; and Stonewall, next to Greenhill and opposite Halliwell Lane, the boundary of Cheetham Hill village. It was at Stocks House that Charles Dickens met the Grant brothers (on whom he based the Cheeryble brothers in his novel *Nicholas Nickelby*) at dinner one night. Stonewall was the home of Thomas Henshaw, a felt hat manufacturer, who left £20,000 in his will for an Institution for the Blind and £20,000 for the Blue Coat School for Boys in Oldham. Strangeways Hall stood in its own park, Strangeways Park, on the edge of Cheetham, looking out over the township. Originally the seat of the Strangeways family, by 1770 the hall had become the home of Lord Ducie.

The population of Cheetham in 1801 was just 752, and as late as 1840 the countryside stretched to Sher-

Cheetham Hill Road, 1905.

borne Street. The rural nature of the place was further attested by Cheetwood (by 1900 an urban village) near Strangeways. In 1849 there were tea gardens in the middle of Cheetwood village where the air was 'sweet with the perfume of roses, pinks, carnations, mignonette... in midsummer the smell of new mown hay... in the orchards, currant and gooseberry trees... pear and apple trees.' Tea would be taken in small summer houses which were set in the gardens.

Cheetham lacked some of the requisite facilities for the mills and manufactories, but, more to the point, a number of wealthy merchants had their homes there because of Cheetham's central position and semi-rural nature, which is what really saved Cheetham from the worst excesses of the Industrial Revolution. Merchants in the 18th century supplied raw materials to cottage workers for spinning and weaving, then collected the pieces for finishing and stored them in Manchester warehouses. The results of this small-scale organised production were sold both at home and abroad. Now the warehouses were full of mass-produced textiles. Ardwick Green had also been a popular place for merchants' homes before the coming of the millscapes.

The Metrolink depot for the new tram system, 1995.

In around 1840, however, all this began to change as demand for housing grew from those pouring in from the countryside to work in the ever-expanding mills. Cheetham was incorporated with the original borough of Manchester in 1838. By 1860 Strangeways was densely populated. The hall and park were now unoccupied and the hall was demolished in 1863. The New Assize Courts, designed by Alfred Waterhouse (who had also designed Manchester's new Town Hall on Albert Square), were built on the site of the hall and opened in 1864. Illustrations of ancient punishments carved into the stone pillars of the entrance to the courts symbolised different forms of chastisement intended to deter criminals. Shortly afterwards Strangeways Prison was built behind the courts and opened in 1868. Rows of small terraced houses stood on former meadow and corner shops replaced market trading. The growth of the metropolis had begun. A contemporary journalist wrote that 'open countryside of the 1820s was a solid mass of bricks and mortar by the 1870s'.

Cheetham is the setting for a strange ghost story. Although the story comes from 1964 it dates back to an earlier time and is featured in *The A-Z of British Ghosts* (Peter Underwood, 1971). A house in Cheetham, the exact location of which is not known, was haunted by 'a child's cries and a mournful whistling... and the apparitions of an old woman and a black figure...'

Mediums were called in and in response to messages which they received 'a search of the house revealed a narrow strip of calico sheeting in a

The Convent of Notre Dame School in 1905.

Cheetham Fold Cottages, Briscoe Lane, 12 May 1950. Terraced housing and cobbled streets were typical of many working-class areas well into the 20th century.

chimney, copies of 1922 newspapers, and a pencilled musical score similar to the tune whistled...'

Subsequently some small bones discovered beneath the kitchen floor appeared to be those of a baby. The police insisted that the bones belonged to a cat or to a rabbit, but they could not explain how they had come to be under the floor or why they should have been buried there. A tantalising mystery for posterity.

By 1862 Cheetham Hill Road (then still called York Street), which ran from Victoria Station to Elizabeth Street, was built up and included St Chad's Church, Cheetham Town Hall, Cheetham Assembly Rooms, the swimming baths with a large clock tower, the Knowsley Hotel, the Northern Hospital and the Great Synagogue. There was also a Spanish and Portuguese synagogue. There has long been a Jewish population of some size in Manchester and today there is a Museum of Jewish History on Cheetham Hill Road in the former Spanish and Portuguese synagogue. Wilton Polygon, consisting of a dozen gracious residences, is built on the site of old stables, centred around lawns and shrubbery. Thomas Street had an open-air theatre (followed in the 20th century by an open-air cinema), a skating rink, the post office, a cemetery and the residence of a medical practitioner named Dr Body. Most of Cheetham was regarded as a genteel suburb in Victorian times and there were several hotels, such as the Empress, the Griffin and the Temple. Cheetham Hill had a Prize Band. May Day was celebrated in some style. Horses were decorated with ribbons, flowers and bells and there were festivities and dancing. Donkey cart rides were a favourite with children who would bring the animals oats and straw from the corn shop.

Whit Week was dedicated to children, and in the last years of the 19th century and the early years of the 20th century there were Whit Walks every year. On the Monday of Whit Week the Church of England processions from St Luke's and St Mark's Churches and their schools took place. On Tuesday it was the turn of the other denominations, which included St Chad's RC Church, the Methodists and the Park Congregational Chapel of the Presbyterians. Wednesday would be Field Day and there would be an outing for all the children to Bowker Vale Farm for tea and games.

Cheetham today is rather different from its Victorian counterpart. The area around and including Cheetham Hill has declined. There is a small modern concrete shopping centre where around half the premises are empty. Strangeways Prison has gained an unsavoury reputation. In April 1990 there was serious rioting in the prison which caused thousands of pounds worth of damage. The area around Strangeways is dominated by what is left of the 'rag trade', with warehouses selling all manner of textiles at factory prices, and by the used car trade. Boddingtons' brewery on Bury New Road has been there for over 100 years and is still thriving. There is now a larger Asian element in the population of around 16,000, rather than Jewish families. There has, however, been an 11 percent rise in the population since 1991 and this may be due to the change in focus of local businesses. Cheetham may once again become a desirable residential area, but it will never return to the days of tea gardens where the air was 'sweet with the perfume of roses, pinks, carnations, mignonette... in midsummer the smell of new mown hay...'

Further reading:
Dobkin, Monty *Broughton and Cheetham Hill* 1984.

Chorlton-cum-Hardy

Brow Farm, Nell Lane, 1938.

Chorlton-cum-Hardy, unlike its Chorlton namesake, was never mill-scaped. As late as 1841 maps show Chorlton-cum-Hardy to have been a delightfully rural area surrounded by fields and meadows with simple descriptive names such as Great Barn Field, Lime Bank Field, Horse Field, Brick Field, Kiln Field, or wonderfully evocative names like Tongue Shaped Piece, Great Raids Bungs, Far Edge Hole, Burnt Earth, and Back o' t' World. The fact that the Industrial Revolution didn't manage to reach 'Back o' t' World', or anywhere else in Chorlton, has meant that some rural semblance has been preserved even into the 21st century. Chorlton is subdivided into different areas, not for political, industrial or economic reasons, but through natural evolution. There are no defined boundaries between these areas so delineation can only be approximate.

The oldest part of Chorlton is centred around the Green, with its well known 'olde worlde' Horse and Jockey public house, and Beech Road, taking in Brookburn Road and Barlow Moor Road. Today Beech Road is the main shopping centre, combining traditional village craft shops with more modern stores. Manchester Crematorium stands on Barlow Moor Road and Manchester Southern Cemetery lies between Barlow Moor Road and Princess Parkway. One of Chorlton's former cinemas (there were

Chorlton-cum-Hardy is often referred to simply as Chorlton. This can be misleading as another Manchester suburb also bears the name Chorlton, or Chorlton on Medlock to give it its full name. Even Mancunians get confused when asked to which Chorlton they refer, looking puzzled if questioned and repeating 'Well, Chorlton, of course'.

Both names are cumbersome in full. Chorlton on Medlock is so close to the centre of Manchester that its identity tends to merge with that of the city itself, and it will usually be referred to by names of major streets like Oxford Road, or by institutions like the universities or the BBC, rather than a separate name. The name Chorlton therefore is almost always used to signify Chorlton-cum-Hardy. The old name for Chorlton is even more of a mouthful: Ceorlatun-cum-Ard-Eea, but the meaning is simple: the settlement of ceorls (Saxon freemen) by trees near the water. However, on some early maps Hardy is shown as a separate settlement. The River Mersey (Maeres-Eea = boundary water) runs along the edge of Chorlton parish and the original settlement was probably either on or close to the water meadows.

Barlow Hall, 1904.

St Clement's Church and lych gate, Chorlton Green, 1910.

Jacksons Boat/Bridge Inn, site of the ferry across the River Mersey, 1946.

Wilbraham Road, 1930.

originally five) variously named the Majestic/ Savoy/Gaumont/ABC, is now an undertakers on Manchester Road. What is sometimes referred to as 'new' Chorlton really developed after the railway station opened in 1880 and encompasses Edge Lane, High Lane, Wilbraham Road, Albany Road and Keppel Road. Then there are The Isles and The Meadows. The Isles refers to the Martledge area, which is intersected by streams and stretches along the railway towards Longford Park, north of Wilbraham Road to Seymour Grove. Clay for bricks used to be mined from open clay pits on the site where Oswald Road School now stands and subsequently a brickworks was built on Longford Road. The Meadows are mostly former water meadows and cover Chorlton Ees (Withington Sewerage Works were situated here), Jackson's Boat (where there was a ferry 'cross the Mersey before the footbridge was built), Back Lane, Hawthorn Lane and the area along the river towards Northenden. Today there is a water park and a nature park at Chorlton Ees reached by an old cobbled lane. Finally there is Chorltonville, the garden estate built in 1908 around Lindow Road (off Seymour Grove) and the Darley Hall Estate. Chorltonville was intended to offer comfortable homes in a country area for city and industrial workers, but Chorlton had become so popular with those seeking to escape the city that Chorltonville became a fashionable and much sought-after place of residence.

One of the oldest families in the Chorlton area until the 1700s was the Mosleys. In 1465 a Jenkyn Moseley was recorded as living at Hough End. Hough End Hall was built of local brick in 1596 by Nicholas Moseley, whose brother, Anthony, lived at Ancoats Hall. Hough End Hall superseded the old moated manor house of Withington, which stood on what is now Eddisbury Avenue. After Hough End was built, Withington Manor became the site for Chorlton Farm; but the old moat was retained. Nicholas Moseley was knighted by Queen Elizabeth I and changed the family name to Mosley for his coat of arms, which he was granted with his knighthood. His grandson, Edward, received a baronetcy from Charles I for support given to the king during the English Civil War. Sir Edward Mosley's coat of arms was later adopted by Withington Urban District Council and then by Burnage Grammar School. Hough End Hall was sold in the 1700s, during hard times for the family, to the Egertons of Tatton. By the first part of the 20th century Hough End had become a peacock farm. Barlow Moor Aerodrome, Manchester's first airport, was built on Hough End Fields and operated during the early 1930s before Ringway was built. The GMC police stables and dog training centre now occupy the site.

Barlow Hall was built during mediaeval times after the Barlow family was granted lands in Chorlton during the 13th century. The hall was rebuilt in 1584 but it was extensively damaged by

Father Ambrose (Edward Barlow), executed at Lancaster in 1641, and it is now home to the estate bell from Barlow Hall. In 1412 the Barlow family built a black and white timbered chapel near the hall, which was rebuilt in around 1520. The Egertons rebuilt the chapel again in 1780, this time with bricks and mortar, and enlarged it in 1837. A Church of England Sunday school was built close by in 1845. The chapel finally closed in 1940 because of frost damage. It was demolished in 1949.

Other churches were built during the 19th century to cater for a growing population and an increasing variety of (seemingly Scots based) Christian beliefs. These include: a Wesleyan Chapel (built 1805, enlarged 1827, rebuilt 1873) whose meeting room was used for day and Sunday schools and is now the Beech Inn; the MacFadyan Congregational Church and school (1879); the MacPherson Memorial Primitive Methodist Church and school (1902); the Presbyterian Church of England (1903); the McClaren Baptist Church (1907); and the Emmanuel Free Church (1909). The ruins of Chorton Evangelical Chapel stand across the Green from the Horse and Jockey. The gateway into the chapel grounds is topped by an unusual black and white bell tower. Churches surviving today are Chorlton Evangelical Church on Beech Road, St Clements on the corner of Edge Lane and St Clement's Road, and Chorlton Methodist Church on Manchester Road.

fire in 1879. However, the Barlow line died out in 1773 and the estate was bought by the Egertons, who already owned Hough End. Where the Mosleys were Protestant, the Barlows were devoutly Catholic. St Ambrose's Church was named after

Hough End Hall in 1952. It was the seat of the Mosley family and was built in 1596.

This tranquil picturesque farming area which became a welcome retreat for faded and jaded city types hardly seems a likely setting for the gruesome murder which shocked 19th-century Mancunian society in the summer of 1876. Charles Peace was a burglar who believed himself to be God's gift to women. In fact he was lame and of a very average appearance, tight-lipped with a wide squat nose. He did not live in or near Chorlton, preferring to commit his crimes at some distance from his home.

Hough End Hall in 1970 (off Nell Lane), used as crown offices.

On the afternoon of 1 August he spent some time walking down Upper Chorlton Road, passing and re-passing Darley Hall, which he intended to burgle that night, but he succeeded in arousing the suspicions of Police Constable Nicholas Cock, who was on street patrol that day. PC Cock was a local policeman with a reputation for being somewhat over-zealous. He followed Peace and challenged him on the corner of Seymour Grove. Startled, Charles Peace panicked. Turning, he shot PC Cock at point-blank range in the chest and then fled. The policeman later died from his injuries. He was buried with great ceremony in the graveyard of the old church on the Green. Two local brothers who were farmworkers in the area, and who were known to have a grudge against PC Cock, were initially charged with the crime. One of the brothers was

Barlow Hall, 1900.

The Horse and Jockey Inn, 1927.

Steam locomotive Black 5 44815, Chorlton Station, 1955.

tried and found guilty. Unusually, however, he was not given the death sentence. This was fortunate because he was able to be set free when Charles Peace, arrested for some other misdemeanour, finally confessed to the killing. His reasons for doing so when he had successfully 'got away with it' are not known, but perhaps there is some sort of 'honour among thieves'.

Chorlton-cum-Hardy is more fortunate than most of the Manchester suburbs in that it has managed to retain something of its former country village self. It was an agricultural economy where thatched black and white timbered cottages were the norm (until around 1880) and social life centred around the village green with its ornate drinking fountain (which disappeared during the scrap metal drive of World War Two) and games of boules. Chorlton was incorporated with Manchester in 1904. Recently, the population has slowly increased, by just under 3 percent since 1991, to around 14,000 in 1998. Although the Siemens factory lies on the outskirts of the township, Chorlton has not been spoiled by either industry or development. Watching children practice jumping their ponies in the quiet fields close to the river is a centuries-old pastime, and it is hard to believe that the bustling heart of the industrial metropolis lies just down the road.

Further reading:
Lloyd, John *Looking back at Chorlton-cum-Hardy, Martledge, Barlow Moor and Hough End* Willow Publishing, 1985

Chorlton on Medlock

Chorlton on Medlock today is, in part, indistinguishable from parts of the city centre. It is bounded by Stockport Road, Cambridge Street, the River Medlock and Hathersage Road, sharing borders with Rusholme and Moss Side to the south, Ardwick in the east and Hulme on the west. The northern section of Oxford Road, where the universities and Manchester Museum are situated, is an important spoke in the central hub of Manchester, under which the River Medlock flows virtually unnoticed. This area, however, belongs to the sprawling suburb of Chorlton on Medlock, which was one of the original townships to be incorporated with Manchester in 1838.

Two-up two-down cottages under the shadow of the mills in James Street, 1895.

Like most other Manchester suburbs, Chorlton on Medlock, or Chorlton Row as it was formerly known, began life as a small country village. Its name dates back to the time of the Vikings when Chorlton would have been known as the village of the free peasants on or by the Medlock. Chorlton Hall was built some time prior to 1644 and was sold as a desirable residence in 1790 for £60,000. At the beginning of the 19th century the population was still only 675; but the Industrial Revolution and building of the Chorlton Mills complex rapidly changed all that. Within 30 years the population had multiplied over 30 times to 20,569. During the next 30 years it more than doubled to 44,795, and by 1891 had reached 60,000, almost 100 times the number who had been living there just a century before. The pleasant little country village nestling alongside the river had vanished forever beneath the dark satanic mills and mean streets full of squalid cramped housing.

Though the original village had disappeared, Chorlton on Medlock's rapid expansion meant that the new outer parts of the suburb remained countrified. However, the inner-city section was dominated by the Chorlton Mills complex, which stood between Oxford Street, Cambridge Street, Chester Street and the River Medlock. This included the Oxford Road Twist Mill, built by Samuel Marsland in around 1803 and demolished in about 1930, and Mackintosh's Works on Cambridge Street. In 1823 Mackintosh developed a process to waterproof cloth using by-products from gas manufacture. The factory expanded into other local mills during the 1840s. During the early 20th century the building between Hulme Street and the River Medlock was to become part of Dunlop.

Narrow grim streets of back-to-back houses in multi-occupation, such as Charles Street, Rosamund Street, Boundary Street or Jenkinson Street, huddled

Workers' housing in Back Temple Street, with a cobbled ginnel for the night soil cart to collect sanitation waste, 15 October 1896.

close to the mill complex. Little Ireland, where large numbers of immigrant Irish workers lived, was tucked into the 'bow' of the River Medlock and bounded by Chorlton Mills and Great Marlborough Street. More refined streets, such as Plymouth Grove (where the novelist, Mrs Gaskell, and her minister husband lived at No.84) or Nelson Street (where the Pankhurst family had their home at No.62), Grosvenor Street and Upper Brook Street, had more spacious homes with gardens in semi-rural surroundings. David Lloyd George was born at No.5 New York Place on 17 January 1863 and in 1918 he was made a Freeman of the City. Tuer Street, Robert Street and Waterloo Place had what Mr J. Hatton in 1854 described as 'free ventilation' houses.

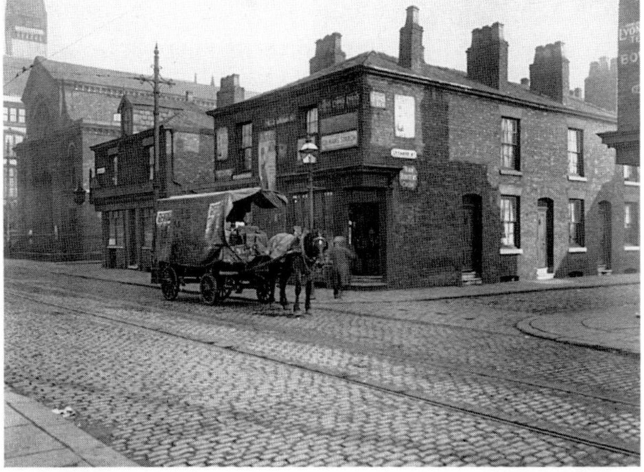

Coupland Street/Lythgoe Street, 26 February 1926. Horse-drawn delivery carts were the norm well into the 20th century.

A row of terraced houses, formerly known as Grosvenor Place, still exists on Oxford Road and today is mainly occupied by cafés, notably the Eighth Day, a wholefood vegetarian restaurant where the old Celtic art of story-telling is revived on a regular basis.

Opposite Grosvenor Place stood All Saints' Church. It was built in 1820, partially destroyed by

Wojtas, wood carver, Downing Street, 1960. The old with the new.

Hulme Street and the dark satanic mills in March 1912.

fire in 1850, blitzed in 1940 and finally demolished in 1945. The grounds are now a pleasant recreational park area which borders the All Saints' Building and the library of Manchester Metropolitan University. All Saints' drinking fountain, a splendidly ornate Victorian creation, erected in 1896, stood just outside the former church gates until 1982. Other Chorlton churches included Cavendish Street Congregational Church, built in 1848 and closed in 1969; St Augustine's, built on York Street in 1908, which was blitzed at Christmas in 1940; Oxford Road Union Baptist Chapel, built in 1842 and demolished by St Mary's Hospital in the early 20th century; St Paul's Church, built in 1862 and demolished during the 1970s and the Church of the Holy Name on Oxford Road, built in 1912 and the only church still standing. Its graceful landmark tower was added in 1928.

Manchester High School for Girls opened in 1874 'to provide for Manchester's daughters what has been provided without stint for Manchester's sons' (Burstall, F.A S.A.). In 1880 it moved from Portland Place to Dover Street. The school was rebuilt in Rusholme in 1940, but was destroyed during the Blitz at Christmas that year. It was rebuilt again on the same site in 1951 and survives to the present day.

Chorlton Town Hall, with its splendid doric pillars, was built in 1830 by the Manchester architect, Richard Lane. Part of the building was occupied by the Chorlton on Medlock Dispensary (established in 1825) and it was also used by the police commissioners and Poor Law officials. Its moment of fame came in October 1945 when the Pan-African Congress was held there. Delegates included Jomo Kenyatta and Kwame Nkrumah. The building was demolished in the 1970s.

Hulme Street on a bitter winter's night, 2 February 1912.

Victoria Baths opened in September 1906 on the High Street, which is now Hathersage Road. The baths were large and imposing, designed to serve Rusholme and Longsight as well as Chorlton. There was a fully equipped laundry and Turkish bath facilities were also available.

Art and cultural recreation were not neglected in Chorlton and this may have had something do to with the fact that there was a strong middle-class element as well as a large proportion of working-class families. In 1898 the Whitworth Art Gallery was opened, funded by a bequest from Sir Joseph Whitworth who had died in 1887. The building was designed by Beaumont but the Oxford Road frontage was not completed until 1908. The gallery remained independent until 1958 when it was given to Manchester University. Whitworth Park, also created by the Whitworth Estate trustees, was opened in June 1890. It had a boating lake, tree-lined walks, colourful flowerbeds and open grassy areas for children to play.

The Bridgewater Music Hall stood on Cambridge Street. The building had a very plain exterior and opened in 1894 as the Alkasar Theatre of Varieties. Subsequently the name was changed to the Empire and then to the Bridgewater Music Hall. It was a music hall until 1923; afterwards becoming a repertory theatre which attracted stars such as Wendy Hillier, Donald Woolfit and Joan Littlewood. By the end of World War Two the theatre had closed and the hall was used as a shopfitters premises. It was eventually destroyed by fire during the 1970s. Bilton's Marionettes, operated by Percy Bilton at his Hyde Grove premises during the 1930s/1940s, were also a popular form of entertainment.

Though the 19th century in Chorlton was

84 Plymouth Grove, home of the novelist Elizabeth Gaskell who wrote North and South *and* Mary Barton, *1959.*

VE day children's street party, Rosamund Street, 1945.

The School of Art in 1890.

characterised by mills and poor housing, the 20th century emphasis was on education and medicine, many of the foundations for this being laid in Victorian and Edwardian times.

The College of Art, established in 1838 as the Manchester College of Art and Design, moved to a new building near All Saints' Church on Oxford Road in 1881. The building was extended in 1898 and today forms part of the University of Manchester and Manchester Museum.

Owens College had opened in 1851 in Richard Cobden's former house on Quay Street before moving to Oxford Road in 1873. Alfred Waterhouse, who designed Manchester Town Hall, designed the new college buildings on Oxford Road on the site of a house in which Crompton Potter, uncle of the acclaimed children's writer, Beatrix Potter, had been born. Beatrix comments on this in her journal during a trip to Manchester to trace her family roots. Whitworth Hall was built adjacent to Owens College in 1902 and the following year both institutions became the University of Manchester. The Students' Union, which had moved with Owens College from Quay Street, was housed in a building on the corner of Dover Street and Oxford Road where it remained until the present Union premises were built in 1957.

Manchester Polytechnic was founded in 1970 as an amalgam of Manchester College of Art and Design (not to be confused with Manchester College of Arts and Technology on Quay Street), Manchester College of Commerce and John Dalton College of Technology, to which were added Didsbury College of Education and Hollings College in 1977 and the City of Manchester College of Higher Education in 1983. The poly became Manchester Metropolitan University in 1992. Shortly afterwards Crewe and

The Unitarian Chapel on Upper Brook Street in 1838.

Alsager College of Higher Education also became part of the Metropolitan University. Today the two universities stretch for over half a kilometre down the west side of Oxford Road while the Royal Northern College of Music lies between them.

St Mary's Hospital (which today is a maternity and gynaecological hospital) was established in 1790 on the corner of the High Street (now Hathersage Road) and Oxford Road. In Grosvenor Street the Adult Deaf and Dumb Institute was established in 1850. Facilities had been in place for children since 1823. Manchester Royal Infirmary, which until 1902 had stood in Piccadilly, moved to Stanley Grove, off Oxford Road, close to the Eye Hospital which had been established in 1814. Today the modern School of Medicine at Manchester University also stands on Oxford Road, not far from the Holy Name Church.

Today Chorlton on Medlock is primarily a place of medicine and learning. How different this is from the mill complexes which dominated the suburb just a century ago. Oxford Road is home to the BBC North studios and extensive new developments by Manchester Metropolitan University. Rosamund Street West, on which the new Metropolitan University faculty of humanities borders, is completely unrecognisable from the street of small terraced houses it used to be where the children played quite literally under the shadows of the mills. The changes wrought in this suburb are some of the most dramatic anywhere in Manchester, but look down along the Medlock from the railway line which runs between Manchester Piccadilly and Manchester Oxford Road and there is still the grim reality of how the millscapes used to be.

St Augustine's Church on York Street, after the Blitz in 1942.

Further reading:
Makepeace, Chris *Looking back at Hulme, Moss Side, Chorlton on Medlock and Ardwick* Willow Publishing, 1998.

62 Nelson Street, the home of suffragette leader Emmeline Pankhurst and her daughter, Christabel, 1970.

Clayton

It is believed that Clayton has its origins in Anglo-Saxon times though this is based on place name evidence and little else. The area would have been occupied during the Romano-British period by local Celtic tribes under the Brigantes, who controlled the north-west prior to and during the Roman occupation, but any trace they may have left behind in Clayton has not been discovered to date. The name Clayton means the tun, or village, on clay soil. The River Medlock, fed by Sunny Bank Brook, which gives its name to Sunny Bank Park nearby, meanders through Clayton Vale to the north of the main settlement of Clayton. Clayton is bounded by Beswick and Miles Platting to the west, Bradford to the south, Fairfield to the east, and borders on to Ashton New Road, on the other side of which runs the Manchester and Ashton-under-Lyne Canal.

Clayton first comes to prominence in the 12th century with the building of Clayton Hall, a moated residence, on land owned by the Byron or Buron family. There is a tragic legend attached to the family which dates from the time of the Crusades. Sir Hugo de Buron set out on the Third Crusade leaving his beautiful young wife at the hall. Time passed and Sir Hugo did not return. Eventually his wife was told that he had been killed in battle. She was devastated and within a few months she died of a broken heart. Her funeral procession was met by a knight on his way home from the Crusades who turned out to be Sir Hugo himself.

Clayton Hall Cottage, still a working farm in 1910.

The tram terminus, 1910.

Clayton Bridge, Nelson Tavern, Muck Dicks in 1928.

Grief-stricken, he renounced his knighthood, surrendered his weapons and gave up fighting. He made a full confession and then became a monk, taking his vows in the remote isolation of Kersal Cell on Kersal Moor.

The hall was rebuilt sometime during the Tudor period. A bell which hangs 'in the wooded turret at the south end of the Hall' was rumoured to have been 'taken from the old parish Church of Manchester during its rebuilding in the 15th century'. Dr John Dee, the Tudor mathematician, alchemist, and astrologer to Queen Elizabeth I, was a friend of the Byron family and dined with them regularly during his wardenship of the Collegiate Church (1595–1604). The Byron family (ancestors of the renowned poet, Lord Byron) remained at the hall until they sold it to Humphrey Chetham, possibly its most famous resident, in 1620. He lived there until his death in 1653. In his will he left money for the foundation of Chetham's Library in Manchester, which was the first free public library in Britain, and for chained libraries to be established in five local churches. He also left money to found a Bluecoat School which was named Chetham's Hospital. Today it is known as Chetham's School of Music.

Clayton Hall survives and is the only example of a moated manor house in Manchester. It had a ghost of course, but an unexpected one. It might be thought that the spectre who haunted the old Tudor building would be that of either the lovelorn Sir Hugo or his wife, or even perhaps Humphrey Chetham, returned to stroll in the grounds of his beloved house. It was none of these but a rather more mundane, if mischievous, boggart. The boggart was finally laid by a local vicar who then declared 'whilst ivy and holly are green, Clayton Hall boggart shall no more be seen'. It remains to be seen

Clayton Bridge, Coates Farm, 1895.

Clayton Bridge, Edge Lane, showing Coates Farm in 1925.

whether, if environmental pollution changes or dulls the natural colour of the holly and ivy, the boggart will return.

Clayton did not escape the ravages of the Industrial Revolution. The suburb was close to the Manchester and Ashton-under-Lyne Canal, which offered easy transporting facilities. There was a chemical works, which polluted the River Medlock, an engineering works and endless rows of two-up two-down workers' cottages with the obligatory public houses at frequent intervals. In 1894 the Newton Heath Football Club moved to a pitch on Bank Street which lay opposite the chemical works and suffered from the chemical plant's toxic emissions. Newton Heath FC became Manchester United in 1902.

St Cross Church was built on Ashton New Road in front of Clayton Hall, obliterating the hall from view. St Cross School was built close by. There was a Board School on Seymour Road and St Willibrord's Church also had its own school. Towards the end of the 20th century Clayton gained an unenviable reputation. The armed response teams for Greater Manchester are now based at the local police station. The population of Clayton, together with

Ten Acres Lane, 1904.

Clayton Barn, an old cruck barn, in 1910.

Action Zone and Health Action Zone initiatives taking place in Clayton, together with neighbouring Beswick and Openshaw, which are described as 'deprived parts'. Clayton is the focus for a new Sure Start programme, which encourages families with very young children to access and take advantage of services and support available so that by the time the children reach school 'they are ready to thrive'. It remains to be seen whether Clayton itself will soon be ready to thrive as well but the signs are good.

neighbouring Beswick, declined by 12 percent to just over 10,300 between 1991 and 1998.

Today Clayton is part of the East Manchester Regeneration scheme and the splendid new stadium built for the Commonwealth Games in 2002 dominates the local landscape. There are Education

Further reading:
Hopes, Karen *Clayton Memories* Clayton Library, 2001
Bentley, Mary *Born in 1896... childhood in Clayton...* Neil Richardson, 1985

Clayton Hall in 1895.

Collyhurst

Collyhurst was known as early as 1322 as a hill made grimy by coal dust, probably at that date from open-cast mining, but its original meaning was a wooded hill. The hill was in fact a red sandstone outcrop (like that in Stockport a few miles away) and it was known locally as Red Bank. Sandstone worked from quarrying on Red Bank was used in the construction of the Roman fort at Castlefield in the second century and in the rebuilding of Manchester parish church in the 15th century and the bridge close by.

Collyhurst had a large area of common land, parts of which survived until 1840. Shortly after 1066 there are records of Collyhurst Common being used as pasturage for cattle and swine. Six acres of the common near the wooded Collyhurst Clough were later used for the burials of victims of the plague, or the Black Death as it was known. Rochdale Road was built in 1806 and during construction work human remains in a lead coffin were found in Collyhurst Clough. Modern scientific research has shown that plague can remain active for hundreds of years and it is horrific to think of cattle freely grazing on land beneath which plague victims were buried.

Around 1650 there was great concern that the skill of archery was in serious decline. A law was therefore passed which required every male over the age of seven years to own a bow and at least two shafts of arrows. The best bows were made from yew, but those made from elm or witch hazel (widely used for its healing qualities) were also quite efficient. Collyhurst Common was a popular spot for archery practice, which had to be carried out at least four times a year by every man and boy. Collyhurst had its own Court Leet, a kind of magistrates court, and it would be here that those who failed to comply with the archery regulations would be brought.

The village grew up around the Rochdale Road area and it was on what became Collyhurst Street (between Rochdale Road and Oldham Road) that Collyhurst Hall was built during the reign of Charles II (1660–85). According to the *Victoria County History*, Robert Leaver held the Manor of Collyhurst

Horse-drawn cart at Herbert Datton's off-licence, Harrowby Street, 1895.

The Old Pack Horse public house, Oldham Road, in 1970. An incongruously placed reminder of yesteryear.

and its hall, along with those of Gorton, Heaton and Alkrington. Robert Leaver was a relative of the Mosley family and Nicholas Mosley resided at Collyhurst Hall. The hall was later sold to Charles Ryder, a cotton manufacturer whose hobby was promoting singing in schools and church congregations. He later founded a Sunday School just off the Oldham Road. A map of 1830 shows the hall and some of its land marked out as building plots. It was a three-storey squarish plain building surrounded by woods. To the south of the hall near Moss Brook were more woodlands, of ash and oak, and a forge. On an 1848 map of Manchester the hall is shown as no longer standing and St James's Church was later built on the site.

In the 18th century part of the present Rochdale Road was known as Back Lane and the village was usually approached via Long Millgate or Ashley Lane from Manchester. Four Lane Ends and Walke Lane existed as early as 1666. Willow Cottage stood on the corner of Cramptons Lane and St George's Road. Opposite Cramptons Lane, Lamb Lane led to Collyhurst Lodge and Whitworth Hall. A smithy

Coronation celebrations for Queen Elizabeth II in Limer Street, 1953.

stood on the corner of Lamb Lane and St George's Road. When the land belonging to Collyhurst Hall was sold during the 1830s some of the modern streets were laid out. These included: Chatham Street, Belle Vue, Arundel Street, Gay Street, Spencer Street, Harrowby Street, River Street, Percival Street, Montague Street and Clifford Street.

Scholes' Directory for 1797 lists one Robert Tinker of the Grapes and Compass Coffee House and Tea Gardens in Collyhurst. Tinker's Gardens, as his establishment was called, lay between Rochdale Road and Collyhurst Road, being approached from the end of Osborne Street. As well as providing freshly brewed coffee and afternoon tea, he also arranged for his patrons to enjoy promenading or dancing to brass bands (except on Sundays). In 1814 a cucumber some 7ft 8in long was grown in the gardens and sent to the Prince Regent (later George IV) for inspection. The name of the gardens was changed in 1814 to Vauxhall Gardens. Robert Tinker went on to become a victualler and died in 1836, but the gardens continued in public use until 1852 before closing. Sometimes balloon ascents took place there; the last being by Lieutenant Gale in 1847. After closure it was discovered that the subsoil contained a soil bed of the type used by iron moulders and it was removed. Subsequently houses were built on the site.

During the latter half of the 19th century Collyhurst began to expand rapidly. Chemical works operated in Collyhurst Clough, a short distance from St George's Collieries in the Osborne Street area, which were now making the place even more grimy from coal dust. Beyond, next to a bridge across Moston Brook, stood a logwood mill and Ellam's ropewalk. Near Dalton Street lay Travis Isle Corn Mill and Collyhurst Dye Works; and there were three or four dye works on the banks of the River Tib. The river ran through fields and 'was very pretty' close to Smedley Road. On Cramptons Lane in Hendham Vale stood the brewery, a cotton worsted dye works and the red sandstone quarries, with Collyhurst Paper Mill standing close to the junction of Rochdale Road. There was a gas works in Gould Street and brick-making on land next to Collyhurst Hall. Craven Brothers' Foundry in Hamilton Street manufactured lathes and other machinery.

To cater for the growing working population that these industries required, houses, schools and churches were built. St James's Church was built on the site of the former Collyhurst Hall in 1855 (the church was closed in 1971 and was demolished in 1972) between St George's on St George's Road (formerly Back Lane which became Rochdale Road) and the Albert Memorial on Queens Road. The Albert Memorial Church, which had seating for 700 souls and was named after the Prince Consort, was built in 1864. It was an active church which held Saturday evening prayer and praise meetings and midweek bible readings, in addition to Sunday services. Like St James's, the church was closed and demolished in 1972. St George's was first built in the early 18th century and was rebuilt in 1877 on Oldham Road. A cleric of the time remarked drily that 'if the Word be sent not for the righteous, but others, the situation of the church is surely ideal'. St George's, however, survived for exactly a century more and was closed in 1977. St Thomas Redbank, built as its name suggests, close to the quarries, first opened its doors in 1844 and closed them again in around 1930. St Catherine's was built on the banks of the River Irk in 1859 and was demolished in 1966. This church was strongly Protestant. During the period 1900–1950 Geneva sermon-preaching gowns (black preaching gowns used by Calvinists) were worn and the Orange Lodges paraded there annually. Meanwhile there was a Roman Catholic Chapel and a nunnery on Livesey Street. St Oswald's Church was built on Rochdale Road in 1855 near the then rural Halls Crescent, where there were some artificial lakes. St Oswald's School opened some 20 years later in 1875 with a roll of 775 children.

Mays pawnshop opened in 1825 on Rochdale Road. Every Monday the little shop, with its trademark three golden balls hanging above the doorway, did a roaring trade as labourers wives queued to pawn their husbands' suits and their own wedding rings (to be redeemed on Saturdays after wages had been received) so that the family would have some food on the table during the week. In Osborne Street there were public baths with a swimming pool, facilities for taking hot baths and a wash house for doing laundry. Terraced houses were built quickly, but often not to very high standards, and slums developed on Rochdale Road within 50 years. However, according to Revd A.J. Dobbs, in his very readable book on Manchester church history *Like a mighty tortoise...* published in 1978, it was the railways which did a lot of the real damage to Collyhurst. 'Railways made heavy demands in Collyhurst, soaring brick viaducts were slung along the Irk Valley, adding gloominess and more pollution to the trapped atmosphere below.' He adds that 'Angel Meadow was transformed from a pleasant suburb to a sordid blackened squalidness.'

John Hargeaves Ltd, Collyhurst Paper Mills in 1966.

Angel Meadow is actually in the city of Manchester, but Revd Dobbs's description sums up the price paid by so many city suburbs for the benefits brought by a faster and more efficient means of transport for both passengers and goods.

Collyhurst has, or rather had, some unusual ghosts. The ghosts did not haunt the site of the Old Hall or the local graveyard, or the lost meadows of the countryside, but a house in Topley Street. The building had been 'used as a spiritualists hall until the caretakers vanished without trace'. It then became the home of a local family with young children. The trouble began in around 1962 when one of the children, who slept in the back bedroom, complained about being woken up by 'an old man in black swinging a watch chain'. The old man was 'later joined by an old woman wearing white who had a malicious look on her face'. Investigators from the Manchester Psychical Society were called in. Tapes were made of the sounds of breaking glass and moving furniture but nothing was actually moved or broken. Animals refused to stay in the house and a budgie was found dead (although without the benefit of autopsy it is impossible to state categorically that this was not due to natural causes). Both Church of England and Roman Catholic clergy tried and failed to exorcise the ghosts. Finally the family could stand it no longer and moved to Miles Platting. What the clergy had failed to do was eventually achieved by a bulldozer when the house was demolished. Who the ghosts were has never been discovered. Mischievous poltergeists maybe, or perhaps the caretakers who disappeared so suddenly and mysteriously. Whatever the truth is, it is unlikely to ever be known.

Collyhurst was incorporated with Manchester in 1885 at the same time as Harpurhey. Today the population has declined: by 12.5 percent from around 12,500 in 1991 to just under 11,000 in 1998. There are modern Corporation housing estates and the suburb is now served by Saviour Church, built on the site of St Oswald's. There is a business park on Oldham Road and a waterworks by the railway. Collyhurst faces the same problems as many of the other suburbs of Manchester, not the least of which are unemployment and vandalism. The quirky picturesque rural little township with its archery practice, tea gardens and community spirit has gone forever.

Further reading:
Now and Then Group *Collyhurst Recollections,* 1993
Barlow, Allan D. *A history of Collyhurst and Harpurhey* Manchester City Cultural Services, 1977

Crumpsall

Crumpsall, formerly a part of Blackley Forest, is mentioned in 1282 as Curmisole and in 1458 as Cromshall. The meaning of the name is a crooked piece of land by a river, perhaps in a valley. Crumpsall Green, which was probably the centre of the old village, lies on a kink in the River Irk showing the early stages of ox-bow formation, which could have led to the name; or the name could have originated from the fact that Lower Crumpsall lies at the head of the Irk Valley.

Corporation flats, 1965.

The mediaeval demesne of Manchester included arable land in Crumpsall but it was difficult farming land lying on the edge of moss and moorland. Crumpsall Hall lay just off what is now Crescent Road and it was here in 1580 that Humphrey Chetham was born. He was educated at Manchester Grammar School and was apprenticed to a linen draper, becoming High Sherriff of Lancashire in 1635. When he died in 1653 he left money in his will for the foundation for a school for 40 boys. The school, known as Chetham's Hospital, was a Bluecoat School for apprentices built on the original site of the Manchester manor house and Cathedral College. Today it is Chetham's School of Music. He also left £1,000 for the provision of what was the first free public library in Britain and another £200 for chained libraries in five local churches.

Joseph Johnson, in his book *Notable Sights in and around Manchester* (1850) writes of 'the pretty village of Crumpsall' and another contemporary writer notes that 'Crumpsall was a pleasant country

Biscuit works on Harpurhey Road, off Rochdale Road, in 1960.

village unspoilt by industry and surrounded by fields in which wild flowers grow in profusion...' Off Springfield lay a house named Ivy Nook and there was 'a small brook in a valley at the top of Springfield in which watercress grew and there were masses of golden buttercups on the banks. In the fields opposite grew wheat, oats, cabbage, swedes and potatoes...' Salmon could be fished in the River Irk. Cows were driven along Waterloo Street to the pastures at the top of Celia Street or to the field at the rear of the Crumpsall Hotel (which later became Cowleys playing fields and subsequently the site of ICI); or to Brown's Farm, or to Jennifer Street for milking; or to Clarksville Farm on Crescent Road. Chadwick's Farm lay down by Bowker Vale Station. In summer hay carts trundled down the lanes and the scent of new-mown hay drifted on the breezes.

Sadly this rural idyll was not to last. While the satanic mills didn't get as far as Crumpsall, the mill-working population did. Between 1897 and 1911, a period of just 14 years, the population of Crumpsall and neighbouring Cheetham more than doubled from 26,000 to 60,000. Today, with Crumpsall's population standing at around 13,000 and Cheetham's population at 16,000, the levels are almost back to those of 1897. Building in Crumpsall began in earnest during the 1860s, as it had in Cheetham, and Crumpsall was incorporated with Manchester in 1890.

St Thomas's School was built in 1850 (and rebuilt in 1898) followed by the building of St Thomas's Church in 1863 and St Mary's Church in 1859. The school stood opposite the CWS biscuit works. Tins of biscuits and boiled sweets were sometimes distributed as gifts to the school, partly as a gesture of goodwill and partly to thank the often boisterous school children for not causing any damage to the biscuit works. In the words of one old gentleman, 'vandalism was unheard of; there was mischief but not viciousness'.

A ruined cottage in 1920 (now the site of Springfield Hospital). Hugh Oldham, who founded Manchester Grammar School in 1515, was born here.

Whit Weeks were a strong tradition in Crumpsall as well as in Cheetham. In addition to St Thomas's and St Mary's churches, there were St Anne's, St Matthew's (destined to become a sledge run site), and Crumpsall Methodist Church on the corner of Lansdowne Road and Oak Road. Each church set its own Whit Week itinerary according to local custom. The Church of England Whit Walks took place on the Monday. Crumpsall Methodist Church then planned the rest of the week. On Tuesday there was a procession which went along Lansdowne Road, Moss Bank, past Woodlands School to the corner of Cheetham Hill Road, past the horse trough at Halfway House on Bury Old Road to Middleton Road, Leicester Road, Crumpsall

A Whit Walk on Crumpsall Lane in 1902.

Delaunay's Road and toll house in 1903.

Lane and back to the church. Wednesday was Field Day at Brooklands near Heaton Park. On Thursday there was a local trip out, while on Friday there was an excursion to Wales or the Lake District.

The huge population increase meant a big increase in the provision of housing and local amenities. New homes and new streets such as Moss Bank Road, Brookfield Road, Sedgeley Road and Whiston Road were built. Crumpsall Lane School was built in 1904 on land belonging to Pendlebury Farm on the edge of Pendlebury Clough. Chudleigh Road and Shardley Road were also built over land belonging to this farm. Cleveland Road had a landfill rubbish tip and a football ground. Charnwood, a large house built on Crumpsall Lane, boasted 21 cellars. Crumpsall Library was initially sited on Crescent Road before moving to the site of a cooperage where the Campbell family used to make barrels. There was a printing works on Robin Hood Street; and there was ICI and the biscuit works. Coal carts serving the biscuit works used Springfield as chain horses had to pull the coal carts up Delaunays Road near Crumpsall Goods Yard because the roadway was so steep. Similarly the fire engine had to be pulled when attending fires and this was usually done by policemen from the police station at the top of Dobroyd Street.

New corner shops sprang up in Lansdowne Road, Edna Street and Moorside Road. Bread was sold by weight and one shop on the corner of Moorside Road and Eaton Road sold freshly ground coffee. In 1905 it was the only shop to do this apart from Kardomah in the city. The shop also displayed a coffee roaster in the window.

Despite all this development Crumpsall managed to retain something of its previous rural community life. There were active allotment associations on Brooklands Road and Crescent Road in the 1920s, and an annual flower and vegetable show. Bands played each evening during the summer in

The Halfway House Garage, Middleton Road, 1968. Petrol pumps replace the drinking fountains for dogs and horses.

Crumpsall Park and on Tuesday evenings a police band played. Children continued to play the age-old

Waterloo Street in 1909. The bridge over the River Irk.

countryside games of duckstone, piggy, leapfrog and touchfinger. Social life tended to revolve around the church and there were concerts, dancing and singing. On Guy Fawkes night large bonfires used to be lit up on Alms Hill and all the children were given parkin and treacle toffee. The present focus of social life is the Abraham Moss Centre on Crescent Road, built during the 1970s and named after a local Jewish businessman Abraham Moss, who had helped to fund the King David High School on Eaton Road in the 1920s. The Abraham Moss Centre combines the Crumpsall campus of City College; Crumpsall Library; a swimming pool; Abraham Moss High School (badly damaged by fire in 1997); and the Abraham Moss Theatre, which includes a black arts company, a special needs company, a youth theatre, a pantomime company and an adult theatre company.

The ICI works with part of Springfield Hospital in the background, March 1974.

Today the suburb remains very built up but it is trying to raise its profile. The Abraham Moss Centre is flourishing but security is obviously tight as a result of the general social problems of the late 20th century. City College promotes the ethic of adult education. The bakers, Slatterys of Manchester, has its works on Cleveland Road and provides local employment opportunities. Further along Cleveland Road there is a school and now a church of St Matthew with St Mary. Crumpsall Park on Ash Tree Road offers a brief reminder of old rural Crumpsall and sometimes it is difficult not to feel an overwhelming nostalgia for the pretty little village it once was.

Further reading:
Crumpsall District Library *A remembrance of things past...* 1972

Didsbury

The name Didsbury is of Saxon origin. *Dyddi's burg* belonged to a Saxon landowner named Dyddi and was probably a fortified manor, the usual meaning of burg, lying close to the River Mersey on the old salters' way from Cheshire to Yorkshire. St James's Church is built on the site of a wooden chapel which was 'of antiquity beyond memory' in 1235. The chapel acquired a consecrated graveyard in 1352 as a result of the Black Death, which decimated Europe. Victims died screaming in delirium and agony caused by huge black boils which formed in the groin and armpit. Death, when it came, was a merciful release. The chapel was rebuilt in 1620 and a tower was added so that it became like the church with which Didsbury residents are familiar today. St James's was extended and rebuilt in 1842 and further restored in 1855.

The Roman well in the grounds of the Old Parsonage in 1900.

Somewhere along the way, a parsonage for St James's was built next to the Old Cock Inn on Spring Hill Lane (now Stenner Lane) to house the clergy who preached in the church on Sundays and cared for the day-to-day spiritual needs of their flock. However, life was far from peaceful for those who lived in the parsonage. They were woken during the night by bells ringing, noises, thumps and bangs which came from within the house. Servants refused to sleep there overnight. Some claimed that they had seen transparent wraiths floating through the trees of the graveyard and the parsonage garden; perhaps the ghosts of the long dead victims of the Black Death. Things became so bad that clergymen of all

The former Capitol Cinema, later the ABC Television Studios, where a number of live shows were recorded, 1959.

denominations were hired to lay the spirits but nothing worked and in 1850 the parsonage was abandoned.

The house became known as The Old Parsonage and lay empty for some time until 1865 when it was bought by local writer and historian, Fletcher Moss. He was sceptical of the claims and described the parsonage 'as having no cellars, no ventilation or lift shafts where howling winds could be mistaken for ghosts'; but Gomer, his terrier dog, appeared to have

Millgate in 1860. A very early photograph.

The Olde Cock Inne, 1900.

other ideas. He would frequently growl at 'something standing in the doorway of the house', his bristly hair and tail standing on end. Fletcher Moss finally decided that 'Gomer's sixth sense had probably detected a prehistoric spirit for which the house had become notorious'.

He doesn't say who or what the 'prehistoric spirit' was, but it would have been someone or something which had been there long before the house was built. In prehistoric times (i.e. before the Romans) Didsbury was a heavily wooded fertile area, through which the River Mersey flowed, and it would have been settled by the Celtic peoples who arrived in Britain around 500 BC. The Celts worshipped trees, water, the earth, all things natural. Their priests, the Druids, invoked powerful passions and powerful spirits. Alternatively the 'prehistoric spirit' may have been an ancient elemental spirit often found close to woods and water. Small wonder that in 1902 when Fletcher Moss bought a fine pair of wrought iron gates topped by eagles from the Spread Eagle in Manchester and erected them at the entrance to the gardens of The Old Parsonage, they became known locally as 'the gates to Hell'.

Fletcher Moss left another ghostly mystery behind him. Researching a book on Manchester folklore he discovered a haunting tale about a house known only as the Swivel House. Each night at about midnight a lady would appear in one of the bedrooms dressed in 'frills and furbelows, powders and pattens [an old fashioned shoe], and a gown of green brocade rustling like autumn leaves...' She lingered by the foot of the bed for a few moments before silently fading into the wall. Legend rumoured that she was the sweetheart of a previous owner who had been a very wealthy man and that she had been walled up alive because she knew too much about how he had come by his wealth. During 19th century alterations to the house 'a secret chamber was discovered in the chimney stack containing the decaying remains of an old chair and table, and chicken bones...'

Fletcher Moss was refused permission to publish

West Didsbury Supply Stores, 1895. The buildings were contemporary. Mock-Tudor finishes were in fashion.

The parish church of St James, 1899.

the story and since then the house has been renamed several times and rebuilt, so that today no one knows its exact location.

It has been suggested that there may have been Roman settlement in Didsbury since the discovery of a Roman coin from the reign of Antoninus Pius near Millgate Lane. This is entirely possible, but without other supporting evidence it is more likely that it was dropped by a careless traveller or a foot soldier from one of the legions. The present settlement, like so many others in the north-west, owes its origins to the Anglo-Saxons, but earlier settlements may have existed. There are references from 1280 to Didsbury Mill, a water-driven corn mill, which stood on the north bank of the River Mersey where there was a weir and a mill race. Over the centuries the mill was rebuilt, the last time being in 1820. It ceased being operational in 1890 and was finally demolished in 1959.

The well in 1931 after the well-dressing, with fresh flowers as thanksgiving for the flow of pure water.

The old chapelry of Didsbury covered the suburbs of Withington and Burnage as well. Common land in mediaeval times was divided between the townships or villages and this is what happened within the Didsbury chapelry. Barcicroft (field/croft where barley was grown) and Cotton Fields are two such areas. Interestingly the word 'dole', now used to describe state benefits, means a part of a field that was shared out for such use. Strip farming was in vogue in mediaeval times, which meant that each

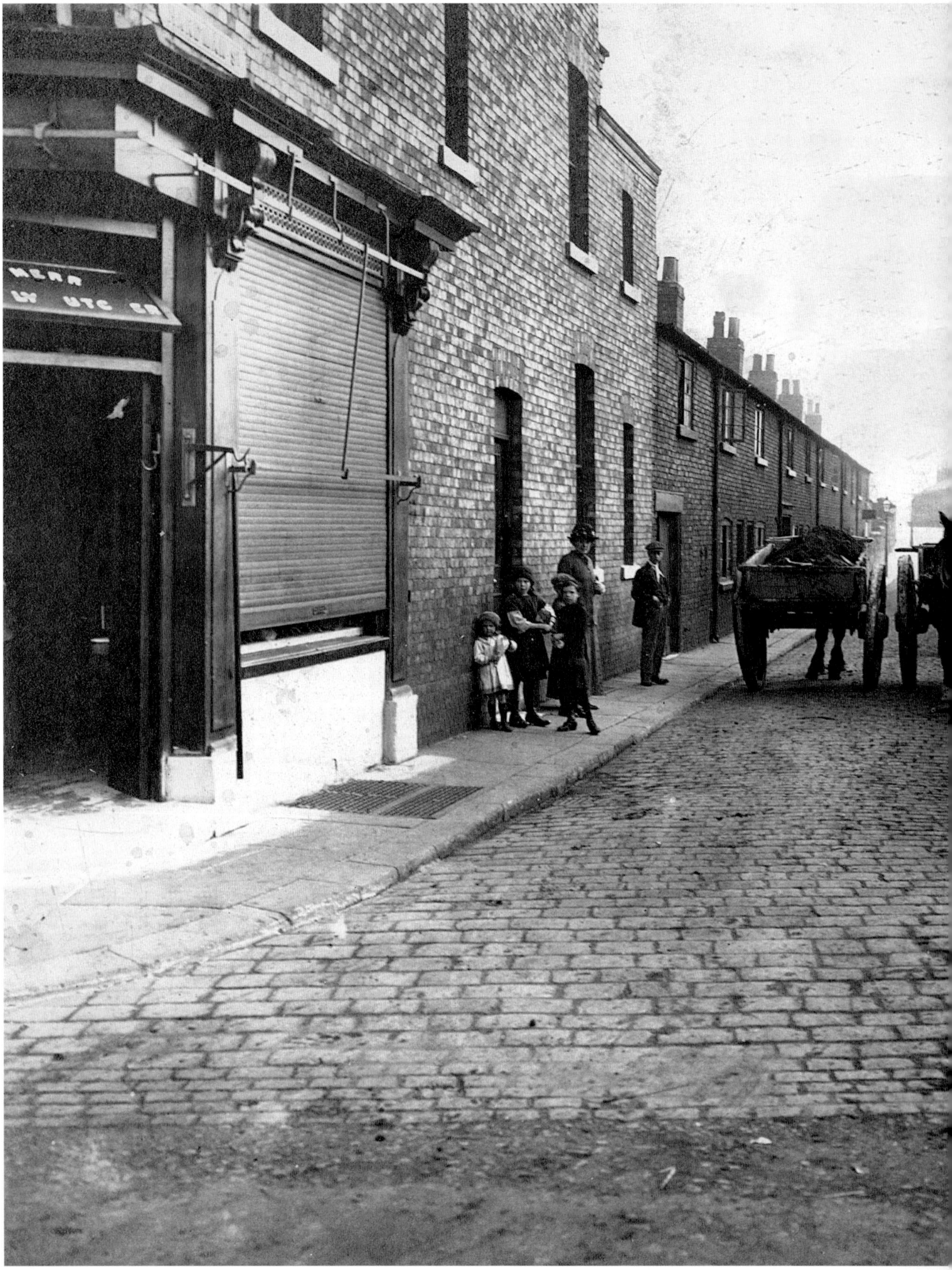

Hardman Street just before World War One, 18 October 1913.

household would have a strip of land within a field on which to grow food. Tithes, a form of rent, would have to be paid in the form of corn, grain, flax, hemp, hay, wool, lambs or calves. Flax, from which linen was spun, usually by the farmer's wives and daughters and sisters, was grown in the Didsbury area and was also imported for the cottage industry from Ireland. On the tithe map of 1845 there are 48 farms shown. Pytha Fold Farm (now Paulhan Road) had the distinction of being the landing place for the first flight from London to Manchester, which took place on 28 April 1910. The plane was piloted by Mr Paulhan, who won a prize of £10,000 from the *Daily Mail* for his heroic efforts. However, only Stenner Lane Farm and School Lane Farm survived the suburban spread of the period 1890–1930. Didsbury, however, did escape the effects of the Industrial Revolution and the population growth was at worst steady. There were 619 inhabitants in 1801 and by 1861 this had only multiplied three-fold to 1,829. Over the next decade the population went up to 3,029; it reached 4,601 by 1881 and 9,234 in 1901;

Lapwing Lane/Palatine Road tram terminus in 1912.

a slow growth rate compared with other suburbs. Didsbury was incorporated with Manchester in 1904. Today, the population is around 14,500, an 8 percent increase on 1991.

In 1752 the Wilmslow Road was turnpiked and there were toll bars at Fog Lane (near Didsbury Priory, which was not a religious institution but a private house) and on Parrs Wood Lane, and a tollbar house stood on Palatine Road. The toll bar on Parrs Wood Lane stood on what became the site of Parrs Wood bus depot, which was demolished in 1988 except for the Clock Tower, still a Didsbury landmark close now to the Tesco supermarket. The Turnpike Trust ceased in 1881, superseded by the Midland Railway which was in turn once again superseded by the roads. Horse buses ran from Didsbury in the middle years of the 19th century before the horse-drawn tram service took over in 1880. Horse-drawn trams gave way to electric trams in 1902 before motor buses took over in 1939. Kingsway was built in 1922. Didsbury railway station closed in 1967, although there is still a station and a rail service to East Didsbury (again near the Tesco supermarket).

The Old Parsonage, whose ghosts Fletcher Moss wrote about, and the parsonage gardens, in 1925.

The focus of population began to shift towards Barlow Moor Road during the 19th century. Several churches were built in Didsbury to accommodate the slowly growing numbers. In addition to the parish church of St James, whose rector established Didsbury Village School in the 1850s, there were Beaver Road Baptist Church (built 1901); Christ Church (built 1881) off Barlow Moor Road and known as the Church in the Fields; St Catherine's; Emmanuel Church (built 1858, extended 1872) on Barlow Moor Road (from where Radio Four's *Morning Service* was regularly broadcast); and Ivy Cottage Church in a cottage on School Lane in 1893.

The last horse bus to run from Didsbury, 1913.

The Marie Louise Gardens, memorial to a sea captain's wife who died tragically young.

St James's, St Catherine's and Beaver Road had schools attached. New 'olde shoppes' were built on Tripps Corner (at the junction of Barlow Moor Road with Palatine Road) in 1900 with a fake black and white frontage to give a Tudor-style effect. There was little industry. Bridgewater Collieries had a yard on the corner of Wilmslow Road and School Lane (then Hardman Street). Provincial Laundries operated from their depot on Dundonald Road from 1911–80. Spann's had a carpet, linoleum and bedding warehouse on Hardman Street (now School Lane) in 1924. Heald's Dairies were established by Mrs Agnes Ann Heald on Ford Lane at Ford Bank, which she bought in 1899. Ford Bank had been the home of Thomas Ashton, a member of the Ashton family from Hyde. Here he entertained Prime Minister William Gladstone and his wife in

The Shirley Institute (for the study of textiles) home of the British Cotton Industry Research Association, at The Towers, 1910.

A procession to celebrate the coronation of King George V in 1910.

Owens Park, a campus for Manchester University, with the Hollings Building, known locally as the 'toast rack'.

December 1889 when Mr Gladstone addressed local Liberals at the Free Trade Hall in Manchester. Ford Bank was demolished in 1934 and a housing estate now stands on the site.

On the corner of Parrs Wood Lane and School Lane in East Didsbury the Capitol Cinema (built in 1931 and rebuilt in 1935 after a serious fire) closed in the 1950s and became the ABC Television Theatre. Here shows such as *Opportunity Knocks* (with Hughie Green), *Armchair Detective* and the *Jimmy Clitheroe Show* were made. In West Didsbury lies Palatine Road, so called because it links the palatine counties of Lancashire and Cheshire. Both counties were 'given power to raise an army and fight without referral or recourse to Parliament'. It is ironic that Cromwell's New Model Army chose the area around nearby Barlow Moor Road to gather for an attack on what are now Manchester's southern suburbs. Palatine Road is home to the Marie Louise Gardens, presented by Mrs Johanne Silkenstadt in memory of her daughter who died on 20 October 1891. Marie Louise had lived at Ford Hall after her marriage until her tragically early death.

Today Didsbury is a thriving student-orientated suburb. Didsbury village is now given over to café society and includes Café Uno, the Saints and Scholars public house, a tapas bar, the Cheese Hamlet delicatessen, a boulangerie, and shops which sell cheap fresh strawberries out of season. St James's and Ivy Cottage Church have survived; so too have Fletcher Moss's parsonage and the gates of Hell. The Old Cock Inn is still there adjacent to St James's, and is much frequented by students on hot summer afternoons. The Didsbury Hotel and the village cross, both in front of St James's and adjacent to the Old Cock Inn, have also survived, and there is now a Didsbury Bowling Club. The UCG cinema complex stands on the former site of Parrs Wood School off Kingsway. The school has been rebuilt behind the cinema and includes a sixth-form centre, a learning centre and conference centre, a sports centre and an environmental centre. Didsbury Library, built by

Andrew Carnegie in 1911 on Barlow Moor Road Corner, is one of only three unfortified libraries in the Manchester suburbs. There is a general air of prosperity in Didsbury and the future looks very positive.

Further reading:
France, Ernest *Didsbury in photographs* 1997
France, Ernest and T.F. Woodall *A new history of Didsbury* E.J. Marten, 1976
Moss, Fletcher *Didsbury sketches, reminiscences and legends* Manchester, 1890
Moss, Fletcher *Didisburye in the '45* Manchester, 1891

The Gates of Hell (erected by Fletcher Moss) in 1905 at the entrance to the gardens of the Old Parsonage.

Fallowfield

Fallowfield is first mentioned in a deed of 1317 as 'Fallafeld', becoming 'Falafeld' by 1417 and 'Falowfelde' in 1530. At least part of the lands were held sometime during the 1300s by Jordan de Fallafeld. Fallowfield has a very literal meaning of fallow or yellowish land and harks back to the rural past of Manchester's suburbs. The exact area of Fallowfield is hard to define, but it is generally considered to be bounded by Platt Brook/Old Hall Lane in the north; Ley Brook/Brook Road to the south; Shooting Gallery/Whitworth Lane on the east; and Mauldeth Road/Wilbraham Road to the west. There is also a section to the north-west which encompassed Dog Kennel Path, Demesne Farm, Dog House Farm and Old Hall Farm. The more northerly 'Rusholme' section was incorporated into Manchester in 1895; the 'Withington' section in 1904.

In the 1820s Fallowfield was still a farming area with trout streams and a few upper middle-class homes, Ashfield, The Oaks, Mabfield, The Firs and Cabbage Hall, set among the open fields. The village store and bakehouse stood on Wilmslow Road opposite Carill Drive. Old traditions, such as well-dressing and the rushcart (now only seen around Derbyshire and its borders), were still practised. Fallowfield rushcart was later used during the Fallowfield Wakes (an annual summer holiday, usually a week in length, during which local businesses and industries closed) when a special rush dance was performed for which all the participants wore clogs.

Although Fallowfield escaped the worst excesses of the Industrial Revolution, its rural nature made it ever more attractive to those seeking to escape city life. During the 1850s new middle-class houses, like Norton House, Norton Villas, Egerton Lodge and Oak House were built. Alfred Waterhouse, the architect of Manchester Town Hall, designed Barcombe Cottage as his own residence on the new crescent-shaped Oak Drive. It was the beginning of the end for Fallowfield as a rural farming com-

Grundy's Farm, Ladybarn Lane, in 1890. The original Ladybarn was a tithe barn named after Our Lady.

The village and the tram terminus just before Wilbraham Road, 1900. Sherwood's Hotel and the railway station are on the left.

munity. Fallowfield railway station opened in 1891 as Fallowfield developed along the Wilmslow Road, which connected Rusholme and Withington. The village store and bakehouse was turned into the Friendship Inn. This building was demolished during the 1960s and the present Friendship Inn stands on the opposite side of the road. Barcombe Cottage became the Barcombe Hotel. The hotel suffered bomb damage in 1941, but although it was repaired the building has now been demolished. Bomb damage also left a huge crater in Cawdor Road in 1940. Oak House, now renamed Beech House, survived and has been converted into student flats.

In the first years of the 20th century most of the farms disappeared one by one. Large Oak Farm and Small Oak Farm on Ladybarn Road were demolished after World War Two. Firs Farm is the only farmhouse which has survived, but it has long since ceased to be a farm. It stands adjacent to the Manchester Athletic Club (MAC) ground which was established on Whitworth Lane in 1891 and included a banked cycle track. In 1955 the MAC ground was bought by Manchester racing cyclist Reg Harris and renamed the Harris

The works on Moseley Road in 1904.

A tram on Wilmslow Road, 1907.

An Edwardian family on Wilmslow Road in 1910.

Manchester Grammar School in the autumn of 1939, with pupils helping to stack sandbags as protection against possible air raids.

Stadium. Subsequently it was acquired by the University of Manchester who built the Owens Park complex and car park on the site. Cycle racing has ceased but the athletics stadium is still in use.

The Holy Innocents Church was built on Wilmslow Road in 1872. St James's was built in 1846 close to Birch Chapel further along Wilmslow Road in neighbouring Rusholme. Holy Innocents was badly damaged by fire in 1954 but the church survived. St James's did not and closed in 1979. After the closure the two parishes united to form a single parish of the Holy Innocents and St James. Educational establishments are diverse and include Holy Innocents Primary School; the prestigious Manchester Grammar School on Old Hall Lane; Mosley Road School (Levenshulme High School, Lower School) used as a hospital during World War One; Princess Christian College on Wilbraham Road; Hollings Campus of Manchester University, known as the 'toast rack' because of its architectural appearance; and a special needs school.

Today the population is around 15,000, a growth of 40 percent in the last 10 years, and Fallowfield is an intensively residential area with a growing multicultural element. A Union Baptist Chapel and a mosque stand not far apart on Wilbraham Road. There is also old and new side by side on Wilbraham Road in terms of housing, and the road is the home of the local USDAW offices as well; a reminder of the continuing fight for the working classes. Fallowfield is clearly a popular suburb and a convenient one for the universities and hospitals of central Manchester, and for this reason looks to be on an upwardly mobile curve into the 21st century.

Fallowfield Jewish Synagogue in 1911.

Further reading:
Williamson, W.C. *Sketches of Fallowfield and the surrounding manors, past and present* 1888.
Helm, Peter and Gay Sussex *Looking back at Fallowfield and Rusholme* Willow Publishing, 1984

Gorton

Gorton, first referred to in around 1282, means a dirty village or farmstead. It may actually have been derived from the Gore Brook, or dirty brook, and the brook may simply have been discoloured by peaty water, or by having a heavy iron content, giving it a dirty appearance. The area known as Gorton used to be in four parts: Gorton village, Abbey Hey, Gorton Brook and Longsight. This may explain Longsight's lack of longevity as an independent entity. The Nico Ditch (or Mickle Ditch), a Danish defensive earthwork, formed the boundary between Gorton and Levenshulme. During the 1300s Abbey Hey belonged briefly to the Cistercian abbey at Dore. Gorton, as part of the manor of Manchester, had passed from the hands of the Grelly family, who were barons of Manchester, into the hands of Sir John de la Warre in 1309 and it was he who gave the land to the abbey at Dore. Hey derives from hay and Abbey Hey was probably the area from which hay was cut to feed the abbey's livestock or which was paid to the abbey as tithes.

The *Survey of the Manor of Mamcestre* (as it was then known) in 1322 states that 'there is the mill of Gorton running by the water of the Gorre brooke, worth 40s yearly, at which all the tenants of the said hamlet ought to grind to the sixteenth grain...' The 16th grain referred to a measure of grinding, beyond the capacity of 21st century reckoning, which ensured that some grain would be left for the miller as payment. There seems to have been a chapel in Gorton from the late 1400s onwards. In 1703 a Dissenters Chapel was built in Gorton Vale. Both chapels were called Gorton Chapel, but in 1755 the original chapel was rebuilt and dedicated to St Thomas. After the Act of Religious Toleration was passed in 1793, and the population explosion caused by the Industrial Revolution, Gorton fairly sprouted churches. There was St James's, built in 1871, which became the parish church; St Philip and All Saints'; the Primitive Methodist on Cross Lane (where the old village cross would have stood); St Francis and the Sacred Heart; Congregational; Evangelical;

Gorton Reservoir c.1900. *A favourite local beauty spot for Sunday afternoon walks.*

The old canal bridge on Reddish Lane, off Hyde Road, in 1912.

Baptists Coverdale Christian Church and the Church of Christ, Scientist, both on Hyde Road. St Francis's, St James's, St Thomas's, and All Saints' had schools attached as well.

The rushcart ceremony took place in Gorton every year until about 1850. Local people would collect piles of rushes at the beginning of each September to renew the rushes laid on the earthen floors of the churches. The rushes were built into a huge pyramid on a cart and decorated with flowers and garlands. The rushcart used to be prepared and decorated in Fox Fold at the rear of the Lord Nelson public house on the corner of Chapman Street and Hyde Road, and was pulled by three horses decked out with bells. Morris dancers accompanied the cart and one Morris dancer, fortified by spirits of a liquid rather than a holy nature, would climb a ladder and sit precariously balanced on the summit of the pyramid of rushes as it made its way to the church.

Gorton Lane became the unlikely setting for the building of a monastery in 1861. The building of St Francis's Monastery was completed in 1867 and the monastic church, designed by Edward Pugin, in 1872. Bricks used in the construction work were made from local clay. The monastery belonged to the Franciscan order, which had also built a chapel school on Gorton Lane. In 1882 the wooden floors of the monastery, warped by the damp atmosphere in Gorton, were replaced with Irish limestone tiles. Gifts of a stained-glass altar window, lady chapel, sanctuary lamp, wrought-iron communion railing, font and a pulpit were gratefully received by the monastery and the church was finally completed in 1885 when the high altar was installed. Surprisingly, Gorton monastery has survived although it is now disused and badly in need of repair. The towering façade of the church with its tiny bell tower still has the power to impress and it remains an enigmatic landmark within the suburb.

The Ashton Canal passes through Gorton and with the canal came Gorton Mills, built in 1852 by the canal side. By 1880 Gorton Mills employed a workforce of 1,550 people. Gorton was also served by the Manchester, Sheffield and Ashton-under-Lyne Railway (opened in 1845) plus the Sheffield and Midland Joint Railway (opened in 1875) which subsequently became the Great Central Line. The Beyer Peacock Railway Works (known locally as Gorton Tank) which manufactured and serviced railway rolling stock, stood on Railway Street. Beyer Peacock began production at Gorton Foundry in 1854. During the next 112 years more than 8,000 locomotives of all shapes and sizes were built in Gorton and shipped all over the world. The steam

ICL on Wenlock Way, 1971.

Woolworth's store in a former billiards hall on Hyde Road, 1959.

Children in a Gorton street, 1900.

locomotives, internationally renowned for quality, safety and reliability, would wait in long rows on the dockside of the Manchester Ship Canal for transportation to every continent. The railway works was a large local employer well into the 20th century. Annual open days were held and the works became a haunt for railway enthusiasts. Beyer Peacock closed their doors for the last time in 1966. Today the buildings are a depot for Manchester Corporation and are used as a furniture stores; but the old railway lines are still visible though partially obliterated through modern health and safety regulations.

Scores of two-up two-down cottages were built to accommodate the large working population. Gorton Baths had a rather ugly red-brick, typically Victorian, frontage. The baths were strictly segregated into male and female. Most workers' homes did not have indoor privies, let alone bathrooms. For a modest sum patrons of the baths would receive a small cake of soap, a clean, if somewhat threadbare, towel and the luxury of a warm bath in a private cubicle. The alternative was a tin bath in front of the fire on Friday nights in full view of the rest of the family. Most public baths of the time had a swimming pool and laundries attached. As the 20th century dawned the laundries offered washing machines and drying facilities. The machines were not the glitzy streamlined models of today, but cantankerous drums which flooded the floor with water. Nevertheless they were a revolution in their day and an important step in the liberation of the female workforce.

There was other industry as well, in the form of a large steel works and the Crossley Works, which made trucks and buses. Gorton had a good market, a Co-operative society and a rapidly increasing number

of shops; plus a number of inns, some with quaint names like Hamlet Falmer, the Rake, Pomona, Unicorn, Dolphin, Cheshire Hunt and Cotton Tree. In 1851 the population of Gorton was just under 5,000. During the half century from 1851 the population multiplied over 11 times so that by 1901 there were 55,417 people recorded as living in the township. Today, at just under 26,000, the population is now half what it was a hundred years ago. Gorton was incorporated with Manchester in 1909.

One of the most popular ways of getting away from their working toil for Victorian and Edwardian Gorton inhabitants was to spend a pleasant afternoon walking by Gorton Reservoir in Debdale Park, one of Manchester's main 'leisure parks'. This beautiful stretch of water was set in picturesque countryside and attracted families, courting couples, those who wanted some precious time in solitude and people who just wanted to stroll and enjoy the old tranquillity which the Industrial Revolution had so abruptly robbed Gorton of. Today the mills and foundries are gone and ICL is one of the largest local employers but Debdale Park still remains off Hyde Road. The park covers some 130 acres and is an unexpected rural oasis which has somehow survived in the middle of Gorton. There is now an Outdoor Centre in the park offering a wide range of facilities and activities that include powerboating, windsurfing, orienteering and abseiling, which would have amazed the Victorian and Edwardian families who promenaded with their children a hundred years ago.

Sadly, however, it will not be for the monastery, or Beyer Peacock, or the beautiful Debdale Park, that Gorton will be remembered, but for a much more sinister reason. On 23 July 1942 a little girl was born in Gorton in a house which stood almost opposite St Francis's Monastery. She attended the Peacock Street Primary School and, later, Ryder Brow Secondary School. After leaving school, she worked for Lawrence Scott and Electrometers, a local firm of electrical engineers, while her fiancé was a tea-blender with the local Co-op. During her late teens she began to crave more excitement than Gorton could offer. She considered joining the armed forces

Gorton Hall in 1890.

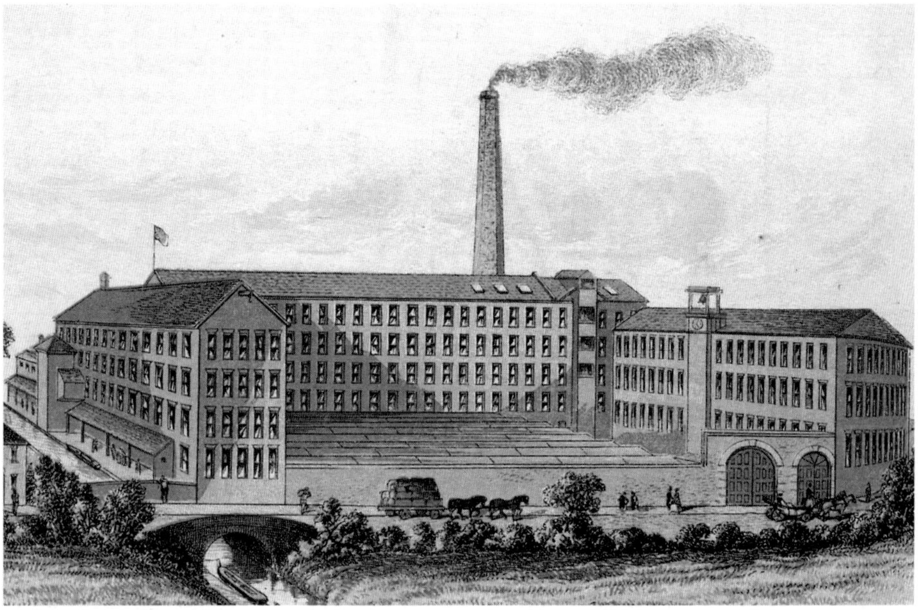
Gorton Mills in 1840.

or working as a nanny in the United States. As it happened she did neither. She met a man who was to change her entire life and earn her a place in the history books.

Myra Hindley believed that she had met her soulmate in Ian Brady and she fell deeply in love with him. They did much of their courting in Glossop, a town some nine miles from Gorton on the edge of the Pennines. Brady and Hindley's kidnap, abuse, torture and murder of a number of children from the Gorton area made international headlines. They killed their victims in a council house on the Hattersley estate (about five miles from Myra's childhood home) before burying the bodies on the bleak and lonely moors above nearby Saddleworth, which led to the crimes becoming known as the Moors Murders. Myra Hindley and Ian Brady were finally caught, tried and jailed for life while Gorton tried hard to forget that Myra had ever been a member of their community for the shame and disgrace that she had brought upon them. Almost four decades have passed but Gorton cannot forget. While Brady has accepted that he will die in prison, Myra Hindley has campaigned relentlessly for her release. If that happens then Gorton will once again find itself under an unwelcome spotlight.

The Beyer Peacock works and steam engine Knighton *in 1875.*

Today in Gorton there are many reminders of the price the township paid to the Industrial Revolution, and there are still heavily industrialised areas, especially around Clayton Lane, Railway Street and Lawton Street. Abbey Hey is mainly an estate of high-rise flats. There is a sports college on Cross Lane and an adult education centre in Varna Street. Another church has arrived. The Temple of the Shalom Christian Church lies on Chapman Street. The Lord Nelson public house still stands off Hyde Road, opposite Brookfield Unitarian Church and school. Peacock Primary School, where the young Myra Hindley went to school, also remains. On Far Lane behind St James's Church there are some cottages reminiscent of an older Gorton and there is now a green and a village atmosphere around the railway station on Lees Street. Gorton is a place where nuances can change rapidly and this is nowhere better illustrated than by watching the timeless scene of a red sunset over Debdale Park on a winter's evening then turning round to the car-park, the lights of a McDonalds restaurant and the roar of traffic along Hyde Road.

Further reading:
http://ds.dial.pipex.com/david.ratcliffe/lhg/vol1/gorhist.htm *Gorton's Past*
http://ds.dial.pipex.com/david.ratcliffe/lhg/vol1/mondevel.htm *Gorton Monastery*

Harpurhey

Mary Taylor's house in 1910. It later became a dogs' home. The local postman stands on the right of the photograph.

The name Harpurhey is first used around 1320 when Sir John La Warre, lord of Manchester, granted 80 acres in the Forest of Blackley to William Harpour, who cleared and enclosed the land. The old English word for enclosure is *haeg* and the area became known as Harpour's haeg. It was very pretty countryside close to Hendham Vale where the River Irk, then 'a clear stream full of fish, ran through woodlands full of wild hyacinths and meadows of daffodils and primroses'. To the west lay Kersal Moor, which was used for horse-racing during the 18th century. Contemporary newspapers record that the notorious highwayman, Dick Turpin, was a frequent visitor to the Kersal Moor horse races, together with his Yorkshire girlfriend, who disguised herself as a boy to avoid being recognised because she was married.

Sometime during the 14th century the Hulton family acquired the Harpourhaeg estate where life continued as a small farming community. As late as 1810 the population was only 188. By this time Harpurhey (as it was by then called) was 'a village of small cottages with grey slate roofs along the tree lined turnpike road used by the daily stagecoach which ran between Manchester and Middleton/Rochdale'. The toll bar was near Taylors Lane (now Church Lane); but tolls ceased to be collected for the Harpurhey turnpike road at midnight on Hallowe'en 1879. Rimmers Smithy lay in Lamb Lane. Samuel Ogden was the congenial landlord of the Golden Lion, a public house and coaching inn which he built in 1794. He was renowned for dressing like a gentleman in Kersey wool knee breeches and serving excellent dinners; and he kept a race-horse named Harpurhey which won the Gold Cup at Heaton Park Races. The inn had 'low white washed buildings, a bowling green, dovecotes, and cooing pigeons' (though the writer probably meant cooing doves) and was clearly very popular.

In 1812 Harpurhey was sold to the Andrew family. The family worked in the dyeing trade and

Central Avenue. The construction of the bridge over the River Irk in the winter of 1909.

their new home suited them well. Crumpsall, Harpurhey, Blackley and Moston were to become a centre for the dyeing and bleaching industries because they were 'too far off and too dry for cotton mills'. For some time there had been attempts to create a new red colour which would hold fast when washed, and Andrews dye works became successful in the production of 'Turkey Red', which didn't run like the old madder reds, and a new fainter-coloured print of lilac. John Andrew, who ran the dye works, lived at Green Mount Place on the Green Mount Estate where Robert Andrew had built Green Mount Hall. Thomas Andrew, who owned a printworks on the banks of the Irk, built Harpurhey Hall on Boardman's Tenement at the top of Oak Bank. The gates and lodge to Harpurhey Hall stood at the corner of Turkey Lane, which led to the Turkey Red dye works near Moss Brook. In summer the meadows along Turkey Lane were let as pasture. The village was surrounded by fields of waving golden corn and the smell of new-mown hay drifted through the warm summer days.

Change, however, was in the air. Increasing industrial activity meant increasing population as workers moved to the area and more facilities were required. In 1822 a Wesleyan chapel/school was built on Green Mount Street and later that year a larger Wesleyan chapel was built on the corner of Mount Street and the turnpike road. A second public house, the Andrew's Arms, was also built. A carriage drive led from Green Mount Hall to Turkey Lane and adjacent to this lay the orchard and kitchen garden of Green Mount Place. The roads were still quite lonely and used by itinerant gypsies drawn to the area looking for casual work, so a 'house mouse' (odd-job boy) was employed to watch the washing hung to dry in the kitchen garden.

1836 proved retrospectively to be a year that was a catalyst for change in Harpurhey. The population had increased almost two and a half times since 1810 to 438, but, although there was a Wesleyan chapel, there was no church. In 1836, Robina Andrew, who had inherited the Green Mount Estate, gave a gift of land on which Christ Church was to be built. Money was raised from gifts and events like bazaars and shows. Harpurhey high society was such at this time that Queen Adelaide, wife of William IV, offered to help with the fund-raising, and was only prevented from doing so by the untimely death of her husband and the accession of Victoria to the throne. Christ Church was completed in 1837; followed by a Sunday school in 1839, which was extended to a day school in 1840.

However, it was decided that a separate cemetery

Rochdale Road (Nos 554–558), on 18 March 1897. The cobbles, or 'petrified kidneys' as they were called, are clearly visible.

should be built for burials from all denominations, not only to serve Harpurhey, but also Manchester, whose churches were fast running out of room because of the population density and high mortality rates among the working classes. There was resistance and downright hostility from the local landowners to this idea but to no avail. The Harpurhey cemetery, known as Manchester General Cemetery, was built close to the valleys of Hendham Vale, Blackley and Collyhurst, and was bounded by the Manchester/ Rochdale Road, Boardman Street, Hendham Vale and Queens Park. The idea was that the cemetery should be a pleasant place offering a spiritual peace to the dead that they had never known in life. It was carefully laid out at a cost of £18,000 and the grounds included a pond and 62 catacombs. At the entrance there were three gateways: the central one for carriages and hearses, one leading to the registrar's house and one leading to the nonconformist mortuary chapel, beneath which were 13 unused vaults. The cemetery was opened on 1 September 1837 by Mrs Walker of Whitehouses, Collyhurst.

Despite the careful planning there were soon problems. The catacombs required constant repair and were demolished in 1854. The pond was drained at the same time. Six cottages had been built on Boardman Street to house cemetery workers but they were poor cheap dwellings (built at a cost of around £77 each) with no yards or sanitation. The rent was 2s a week. To add insult to injury the tenants were evicted in 1867 to save poor rates, although the cottages were not demolished until 1881. In 1854 a strangers' vault had been built in the cemetery although its purpose was uncertain. If it was to receive strange interments then it certainly fulfilled its purpose one summer's day in 1868.

Miss Hannah Beswick of Birchin Bower, Hollinwood, died at Cheetwood Hall in Manchester in 1785. She had an absolute horror of being buried alive and so she left her doctor a sum of money on the condition that she was never buried below ground. Her body was embalmed by Dr White, a founder of Manchester Infirmary, and initially she was kept at Ancoats Hall, where a member of the Beswick family lived. Perhaps the family found this too gruesome, for shortly afterwards she was removed to a specially constructed room at the top of the Priory in Sale, the residence of Dr White. After his death her body was placed in the care of

Queens Park Museum, Queens Park, in 1900.

Laundry service in 1920.

Dr Ollier, and was subsequently given to the old Manchester Museum in Peter Street where she became known as the 'Manchester Mummy'. When the Manchester Museum was transferred to Manchester University a meeting of the trustees and medical representatives was held to decide what should be done with 'the Mummy of Birchin Bower'. They took into account her wishes and her pathological fear of being buried alive, but decided that, after 93 years, she was 'irrevocably and unmistakably dead'. Consequently she was buried in the Harpurhey cemetery on 12 July 1868.

Harpurhey continued to increase in size, industry and population. The dye works was followed by engineering works, rope works, tarpaulin works, wire works, two mills and a brewery. The brewery

Central Avenue. The construction of bridge over the River Irk, 10 May 1910, against the backdrop of the millscapes.

Coronation celebrations for Queen Elizabeth II on Walter Street, 1953.

was founded by John Collinson and George Simpson and became Wilson's Brewery, which was bought by Watney Mann in 1960. St James's Chapel, with its octagonal spire, was built by Frank Newby in 1855. Queens Park was created within the grounds of Hendham Hall (demolished 1884) in 1845 and given to the city of Manchester the following year. After the fashion of the day Queens Park also had an art gallery and a museum; and a statue was erected in the grounds to the 19th-century north Manchester poet and dialect writer, Ben Brierley. Harpurhey was finally incorporated with Manchester in 1885. The little country village had gone forever. Its passing did not go unnoticed. Philip Wentworth thundered in the *Middleton Guardian* of 29 January 1885 against the 'desecration of the countryside, the famous oaks of Moston, all the farmsteads, the pretty countryside of Harpurhey...' He placed the blame fairly and squarely on James Watt and his steam engine.

Over a century later it is difficult to disagree with Mr Wentworth and his view of the damage done by the Industrial Revolution to the suburbs of Manchester. In 1998 Harpurhey had a population of just under 11,000, a decline of 8 percent on the population census taken in 1991. The area has suffered, in common with many of the other Manchester suburbs, from the increasing traffic, the throw-away society and the yob culture of the late 20th century; although it would seem that yob culture was also a problem for the 19th century as well, with one writer on Harpurhey in 1836 complaining of 'the drunkenness in slum-urbia'! Harpurhey Library looks like something out of *Star Wars* and, like most of the district libraries in Manchester, it is heavily fortified. Sadly that has become the fate of many public buildings in the city suburbs. It is hard to read the description of Harpurhey in 1810 without experiencing an unbearable nostalgia for things past, but life can only go forward and perhaps a more environmentally conscious generation will give Harpurhey a better future.

Further reading:
Barlow, Allan D. *A history of Collyhurst and Harpurhey* Manchester City Cultural Services, 1977

Hulme

Hulme takes its name from the Danish for a small island or piece of dry ground in a marsh. Built on the banks of the River Irwell, Hulme is surrounded on three sides by water; that of the Rivers Irwell, Medlock and Cornbrook. It was probably originally a settlement on an area of slightly higher dry ground set in the converging water meadows of the three rivers.

Condemned housing in 1962.

Early Hulme was romantic enough. A small farming settlement by the river in the days of the Vikings, it had grown into a village in which agriculture was the main occupation by the 18th century. The village had its own manor house, Hulme Hall, a splendidly picturesque black and white timbered building with gables at every turn, giving it the appearance of a storybook haunted house. However, the hall was not haunted in the ordinary sense of someone who had died tragically or who was wandering about looking for a long-lost love. A 19th-century writer describes the hall rather darkly as having 'unearthly guardians, demon charms' who prowled the grounds in sinister fashion guarding the secret location of a buried treasure.

The legend surrounding Hulme Hall is one to be told on a dark winter's night by the light of a flickering candle. The exact age of the hall is unknown but Adam, son of Adam of Rossendale, was living there during the reign of Edward I (1272–1307). It then came into the ownership of the Prestwich family. During the Civil War (1642–51) Sir Thomas Prestwich, encouraged by his mother, supported King Charles I. The Lady Dowager induced her son to part with considerable sums of money to the Royalists on the promise that she had hidden a great deal of treasure in the grounds of the hall. The legend says that she protected this treasure by means of spells and magic, but before she could tell her son of its whereabouts she was struck by a mysterious illness, which rendered her dumb and immobile, and she died without revealing her secret.

In victory the Parliamentarians vented their anger on Sir Thomas for supporting the king. He was fined heavily and part of his estate was confiscated. Impoverished, he mortgaged the hall to Nicholas Mosley of Ancoats, who finally bought it outright in 1673. Despairingly, Sir Thomas searched in vain for the treasure but he never discovered where it lay hidden and he died in great poverty. The hall briefly became the property of the Bland family but in 1764 (the year the Bridgewater Canal was completed) it was purchased by the Duke of Bridgewater. By 1845, however, the building was in a dilapidated condition and was demolished to make way for the railway. Just before demolition several panels of grotesque wooden

Bomb damage caused during the Blitz, 24 June 1940.

figures were removed from the hall and taken to Worsley Hall. Were these likenesses of the 'demon charms' that the Lady Dowager had set to guard her treasure? During the 18th and early 19th centuries tales of the buried treasure had become so well known that unscrupulous fortune tellers would cheat the unwary out of their money by claiming to know where the treasure lay. However, the treasure remains undiscovered to this day. The 'unearthly guardians' have done their job well.

The comparative rural idyll of Hulme, where 'the white bells of Galatea's lovely convolvulus' bloomed in summer, was brought to a brutal end by the Industrial Revolution. Where once the white convolvulus bells had nodded in the summer breezes, the rails of the Cheshire Lines ran roughshod across the land. Mills were built alongside the rivers, the largest of which was the Knott Mill Iron Works on the bank of the River Medlock. Their dark bulk blotted out much of the sky and black smoke belched continuously from their tall chimneys. Street upon street of narrow, cramped, badly constructed back-to-back houses covered the once green meadows. The population of Hulme increased from 1,677 in 1801 to 26,982 in 1831. This number almost tripled in 1831–41, and then the population doubled again from 1841–51.

St George's Tennent in 1986 and an expression of the millscapes in modern art form.

The sheer pressure of people moving into the area meant that builders tried to fit in as many houses as possible and this led to the creation of the infamous courts. Houses were built around a small square which had washing and sanitation facilities in the centre. There are recorded instances of more than 300 people having to share one toilet. Often a whole family lived in one dark, dank room. Basement dwellings were frequently soaked with untreated effluent which seeped through the floor from the inadequate sewage and drainage system. After 1844 Manchester borough council was able to prohibit the construction of back-to-back houses or dwellings without adequate facilities, but daily living must have been a nightmare for many of those early mill-working families. During the years following 1844 ash pits and privies were built onto the sides of houses (often with an extra bedroom above them) and ginnels ran between the backs of houses so that the 'night soil cart' could collect the waste. In 1844 Friedrich Engels described Hulme as 'one great working people's district'. He walked many of the streets in Hulme and wrote movingly of the appalling conditions which the working classes were forced to endure.

The rapid increase in population density meant the building of facilities such as schools, churches, libraries, public baths and washhouses. Several churches, often with schools attached, were built but only St George's, St Wilfrid's and the Zion Chapel have survived, and of these only St Wilfrid's is still used as a church. St George's was the church for Hulme Barracks. The barracks, built in 1817, were used by the cavalry until 1895 and then by the infantry until 1914 when most of the barracks were demolished by Manchester Corporation. There was a free library on Chester Road, one of the first in Manchester, with a special reading room set aside for children. Hulme Branch Library opened in 1866 next to the Town Hall (built in 1865) on Stretford Road. Hulme Lads Club had a membership of 2,000 during the first couple of years after it was set up. On Leaf Street the Leaf Street Baths were completed in 1860. This large Victorian edifice housed swimming baths, plunge baths and a laundry with washing machines and spindryers, although these were not of a type to excite modern housewives or husbands since they were not automatic and left plenty of water on the floor.

One of the most remarkable and unlikely creations to come out of Hulme was the Rolls-Royce car. In 1904, Henry Royce, an electrical engineer, and Charles Rolls, a car salesman, met at the Midland Hotel in Manchester, as a result of which the first Rolls-Royce motor car was born in a Hulme back street in 1905. By 1906 the company had established works in Cooke Street. A 10 horsepower car cost around £400 while a top-of-the-range 30 horsepower car sold for about £900. The company moved to premises in Derby in 1907. At the other end of the spectrum real horsepower continued to be used for transport in Hulme as late as 1960. There was still a working blacksmith on Dumblane Street in 1957.

Boundary Street West in 1964. This was part of the area of Hulme which was redeveloped.

Hulme suffered heavy damage in the Blitz of 1940, particularly in the Chester Road/Stretford Road area, and in air raids throughout World War Two. Nearly 2,000 houses were destroyed while a further 50,000 properties needed repair. Stretford Road, linking Oxford Road and Chester Road, was one of the main roads in Hulme. Queen Victoria rode along it on her way to open the Manchester Ship Canal in 1894; as did King Edward VII when he opened No.9 Dock in 1905. Great Jackson Street

also linked Stretford Road with Chester Road and it was crossed by City Road, which traversed the Hulme district. Both of these thoroughfares followed old country lanes and tracks though there is little trace left now of Hulme's rural past. However, on Embden Street in 1932 there stood a row of cottages completely covered in thick creeper, a brief reminder of the vanished countryside.

In 1955 the Playhouse (built in 1902; formerly named Hulme Hippodrome and then the Grand Junction), which could seat an audience of 1,500, was taken over by the BBC for recording variety shows. These shows are no longer popular and the Playhouse has fallen into disuse. Hulme Hippodrome (formerly a music hall built in 1901 and initially named the Grand Junction) could seat 3,000 people and Victorian melodramas were performed there. Around 1905 interest in melodramas began to decline as other forms of entertainment were introduced. Music hall, however, retained its popularity and it was at this point that the two theatres changed names. The Grand Junction became Hulme Hippodrome, and continued to put on music hall shows, while the smaller theatre became the Grand Junction and later the Playhouse.

By the 1960s large-scale slum clearance had been undertaken in Hulme and new crescent-shaped blocks of flats were built according to contemporary architectural and social ideals. They were completely soulless and helped to destroy the vibrant community life of the area so evident in the street parties held to celebrate the coronation of King

Stretford Road, near Henry Street, on 1 November 1910.

Hulme Hall in 1833, against a backdrop of encroaching millscapes.

Lower Ormond Street. Policemen helping schoolchildren to cross the road in 1900.

George VI in 1937. Hulme Crescents became notorious for poverty and crime and they were eventually demolished in the early 1990s to make way for the more individual style of housing which they had replaced. Today the Crescents are just a folk memory and a topic of study for local A-level students.

Hulme of the 1960s was an unlikely setting for a ghost story but in 1963 a ghost known as the 'Foxtrot Phantom' terrorised Alderly Street. The ghost first began knocking and banging in a foxtrot rhythm on New Years Eve 1962 at the home of the Miles family. This continued every night for the next six months. The knockings vibrated through several of the terraced houses and inch-wide cracks appeared in the street. Residents were terrified. Police and council officials could not trace the cause. Eventually psychical research experts were called in but failed to identify the ghost. Tantalisingly, 40 years on, there is still no explanation as to who or what the Foxtrot Phantom was.

The current population figures are about 9,700, an increase of over 25 percent in last 10 years. St George's is at the centre of a redevelopment area.

The Three Legs of Man public house on Stretford Road, 1880.

There is a new shopping complex and a medical centre and some very upmarket canal-side flats in converted industrial buildings. The Kingdom Revival Ministries are situated near Greenheys Lane. However, Hulme is still an area of social deprivation and loss of community spirit and as the 21st century dawns the suburb is experiencing troubled times of a nature not known during the days of the millscapes.

Further reading:
Makepeace, Chris *Looking back at Hulme, Moss Side, Chorlton-on-Medlock and Ardwick* Willow Publishing, 1995.

A motorbike and sidecar with three young women, 1920.

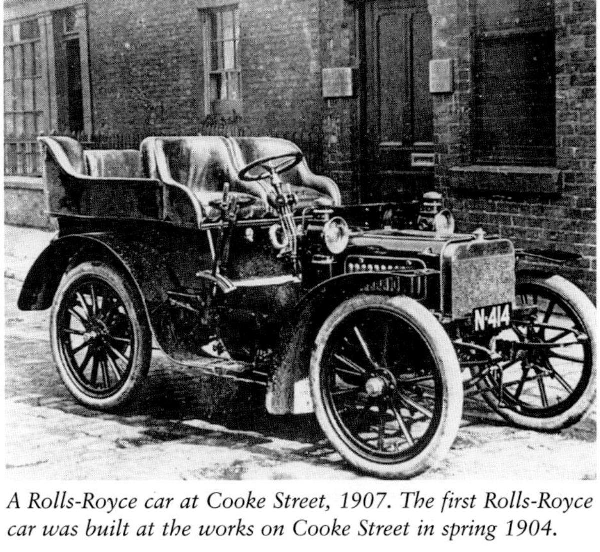

A Rolls-Royce car at Cooke Street, 1907. The first Rolls-Royce car was built at the works on Cooke Street in spring 1904.

Levenshulme

Levenshulme is bounded by some rather unusual and romantic sounding features: Nico Ditch, Pink Bank Lane, Cringle Brook, Slade Lane and Burnage Lane. Hulme comes from the old Danish word *hulm* or *holm* meaning an island. Levens is a corrupted form of Leofwine, an unknown Dane who gave his name to this 'island' which he had been granted. There have been a variety of spellings for Levenshulme over the centuries. In the Manchester survey of 1322 it was listed as Lywensholme. By 1556 the Collegiate Church Charter was calling it Leysholme, followed by Lensholme in 1578 and Lentsholme in 1635. In Tudor and Stuart times, however, spelling was very much a matter of taste for individual writers. Today the pronunciation of the name is pretty much as it was back in 1322.

The Nico Ditch was a defensive earthwork against the Danes, or Vikings as they came to be called in the 19th century. The ditch failed in its original purpose since the whole area eventually came under the Danelaw, but it was an impressive feature running from Ashton Moss in the south west, through Rusholme to Hough Moss. Parts of it were still visible until the early 20th century in Levenshulme as a watercourse between St Oswalds Road and Mount Road (near Stockport Road). There is a preserved section in Platt Fields park opposite Old Hall Lane in Rusholme.

An old rural cottage in 1885.

A gypsy caravan near the railway in 1905.

By the 13th century Levenshulme had become part of the Slade Estate held by the Slade family, but in 1558 Richard Siddall, from Withington, purchased the lease, and by 1584 the Siddalls owned the estate outright. Slade Hall was rebuilt by Edward and George Siddall in 1585 and their initials, together with the date, are carved over the main doorway. The hall is a black and white timbered building with an oak framework, 3ft-thick internal walls, rushes/plaster infill and square mullioned windows. The hall remained in the Siddall family until 1903, when John Siddall sold it, along with part of the estate, to the London and North Western Railway Company.

Levenshulme formed part of the Heaton Chapel parish and the 'local' church was St Thomas's, built in 1765, on Wellington Road North in Heaton Chapel. Old farms and houses shown on Johnson's map of Levenshulme in 1820 include Midway House, Church Farm (now site of Barclays Bank), a small chapel on Chapel Street, Black Brook Farm, Slade Hill, Slade Hall, Cringle Cottage, Craddock Fold, the quaintly named Botany Bay Cottage, Hurst Farm and the Bull Inn. There was a smithy in Matthews Lane and another one in John Street (now Jean Close). The Leghs of Baguley also owned land in the district though they sold some of it during the 18th century to form part of the endowment of Gorton Chapel.

Barlow Road was known as Talleyrand Lane between the present public library and Pink Bank Lane, while the Stockport end of the road, opposite Yew Tree Farm, was Adlands Lane. The Old Blue Bell Inn on Barlow Road (near Lincoln Avenue) was reputed to be over 700 years old in 1910 and its cruck roof timbers gave some credence to this story. There is also a legend that Dick Turpin was 'a regular' there. Newspaper reports from 1737–8 state that he attended Manchester Races several times so there is a chance that there may be some truth in the legend. Levenshulme was just another quiet country village, in which agriculture was the main occupation, before the sprawling tentacles of the Industrial Revolution reached out to engulf it. Amazingly, as late as 1844, 96 percent of the land was still meadow and pasture and only 1.5 percent

The tram terminus in 1910.

Newsagents on Barlow Road, 1909. Newspaper billboards advertise the news stories of the day.

of land had buildings upon it. The remaining land was ploughed and cultivated. Tithes were paid to the Collegiate Church in Manchester. In 1655 there were 25 people paying rates. The main Stockport Road was turnpiked in 1724 and by 1774 the population had risen to 280. Longsight toll bar stood at the corner of Slade Lane but there was no toll bar in Levenshulme since there was no access to the road there from other villages.

The building of the railways marked the end of the farming community because land was required for houses to accommodate the boom in urban population increase, particularly from the 1880s onwards. In 1881 Levenshulme Urban District Council (UDC) was formed and took over from the Levenshulme Board of Health, which had been established in 1865. Levenshulme Town Hall was built in 1898 by the UDC with the police station next door. Due to the comparatively late urbanisation of Levenshulme and the standards set by the UDC, housing built in Levenshulme was of superior quality and in less density than that in other suburbs. Rushford Park was a leafy housing estate linked to Stockport Road by the Crescent, and

Birchfields Road on 26 February 1906. A last glimpse of rural Levenshulme.

Burnage Lane in 1910. It is now a busy thoroughfare.

Cringle Brook, which was a local beauty spot, 1910.

Grange Avenue off Slade Lane had gracious semi-detached houses with equally gracious names like the Limes and the Beeches. Rents on the Crowcroft Park Estate ranged from 5s 6d to 7s per week. All terraced houses had front gardens and back yards and Levenshulme had one of the lowest death rates in the country.

Levenshulme escaped for the most part the curse of the mills, though there was a 'cotton manufactory' in Crowcroft Park. There were, however, other forms of industry. There was a bleach works on Pink Bank Lane (at which point Levenshulme Brook was dammed to supply the works with water) and a printworks near Mounts Road; light engineering works on Manor Road, Chapel Street and the south end of Stockport Road; and, after World War Two, Jackson's Brickworks stretched along the clay deposits which ran from the tripe works to the

Stockport Road on 23 April 1904. Today this road is the main A6 and is often gridlocked with traffic.

southern end of Cringle Road. The tripe works stood close to the railway and thrived during the days when raw tripe and onions was considered a great treat. Tripe, the part of the stomach of cow, sheep or oxen which is edible, is not much to modern tastes. Levenshulme now has a thriving multicultural community, with Indian and Chinese shops and restaurants, and Friday night supper is more likely to be a good curry or sweet and sour rather than tripe and onions.

St Peter's Church, on the corner of Barlow Road and Stockport Road, was built with money provided by Charles Carill-Worsley (of Platt Hall in Rusholme) while Thomas Carill-Worsley built St Peter's School in 1854. The church lych gate was used as a memorial to those who died in World Wars One and Two. St Peter's School closed in 1982 but reopened in 1986 as Levenshulme Islamic Centre. Crowcroft Hall, built in around 1840 in Crowcroft Park, served as the rectory from 1889–1923 for St Agnes's Church on the corner of Hamilton Road and Slade Lane. The Congregational Church was built on the site of former Sunday school buildings on Stockport Road (a new school was built in around 1905), and the Wesley Methodist Church stood on the corner of Wesley Street (now Woodfold Avenue). The Primitive Methodist Church was built of corrugated steel and was known as the Tin Chapel. It stood on the corner of Cromwell Grove and Mercer Street. After closure the chapel became a film studio but was demolished in the years following World War Two. In 1903 the Chapel Street School opened. It was also built of corrugated iron and consequently became known as the Tin School. St Mark's Church, built in 1907, stood on the corner of Barlow Road and St Mark's Street, while St Mark's Rectory stood on the corner of Barlow Road and Printworks Lane. St Mark's School stood on the section of Barlow Road formerly known as Talleyrand Lane, while Levenshulme High School for Girls was built on the site of High Farm at the end of Crossley Road (formerly High Lane/Cow Lane).

Levenshulme Mechanics Institute and Schools were built on the corner of Mayfield Road (now Mayford Road) in 1890. Such schools were often the only source of adult education for working-class adults and proved themselves to be forerunner of the idea of lifelong learning. Levenshulme Library opened in 1903. It was a Carnegie library like Didsbury, built with money provided by Andrew Carnegie. He, however, had helped to suppress trades unions in the United States so his funding gestures were not particularly welcome. After the Boer War had ended in 1902, and before the start of World War One in 1914, there was a period of high unemployment in the Manchester area. The city therefore undertook an extensive public works programme which included projects such as the laying out of Platt Fields Park. Around 1908 a camp for the unemployed was set up in Levenshulme to encourage the work ethic and offer some usefulness and structure to the lives of those without jobs. The camp was run on military lines and the

Slade Hall, on the Longsight border, built in 1585 and still well-preserved today, on 21 January 1903.

inmates lived in military style, working as labourers during the day.

From 1915–38 Marks and Spencer ran a 'penny bazaar' on the corner of Carill Grove East with Stockport Road. Helms Dairy opened for business in around 1920 on the corner of Barlow Road and Molyneux Road, followed in 1945 by Dobsons Dairies in Lloyd Road. A number of shops were built on Byrom Parade close to Byrom House. Near the Midway House pub on Stockport Road a shop had been built across the Nico Ditch. One day, so the story goes, the floorboards gave way and the shopkeeper fell into the ditch. The Midway House was built in 1605. Although vegetarianism is generally considered a phenomena of the later 20th century, the Vegetarian Society was first formed in 1847 and held its meetings at the Midway House. In 1902 the pub was rebuilt in mock Tudor style and renamed the Midway Hotel. Another old hostelry on Stockport Road, the Pack Horse, had mounting steps for horse riders in front of the pub until it was rebuilt in 1907. Apart from a number of public houses, such as the Railway Inn on Stockport Road, the Church Inn on Yew Tree Avenue, and the Wheatsheaf on Stockport Road, leisure was well catered for in Levenshulme. In 1904 Levenshulme Cricket Club was formed and the cricket pitch was bounded by Slade Lane, Park Grove and the railway. There were also several cinemas: the Grand Cinema built in 1922 which became a temporary church for the congregation of St Mary of the Angels and St Clare in 1957 before becoming an antique dealers; the Kingsway Super Cinema built in 1929 and demolished in 1970, and the Regal Cinema, which in 1959 became a bowling alley and then a bingo hall. On Yew Tree Avenue, the Arcadia had a mixed history. Built as a skating rink it became a cinema then a warehouse and finally a sports hall. During the skating rink period a 'Grand Hockey Match' was played between the Arcadia's home team and Fred Karno's team from the Kings Theatre in Longsight. Charlie Chaplin and Stan Laurel were both members of Karno's team.

Levenshulme was incorporated with Manchester in 1909. Today Levenshulme's population is a little over 13,000. Stockport Road (the A6) thunders with

The Blue Bell Inn in 1910. It was an old inn with cruck construction beams.

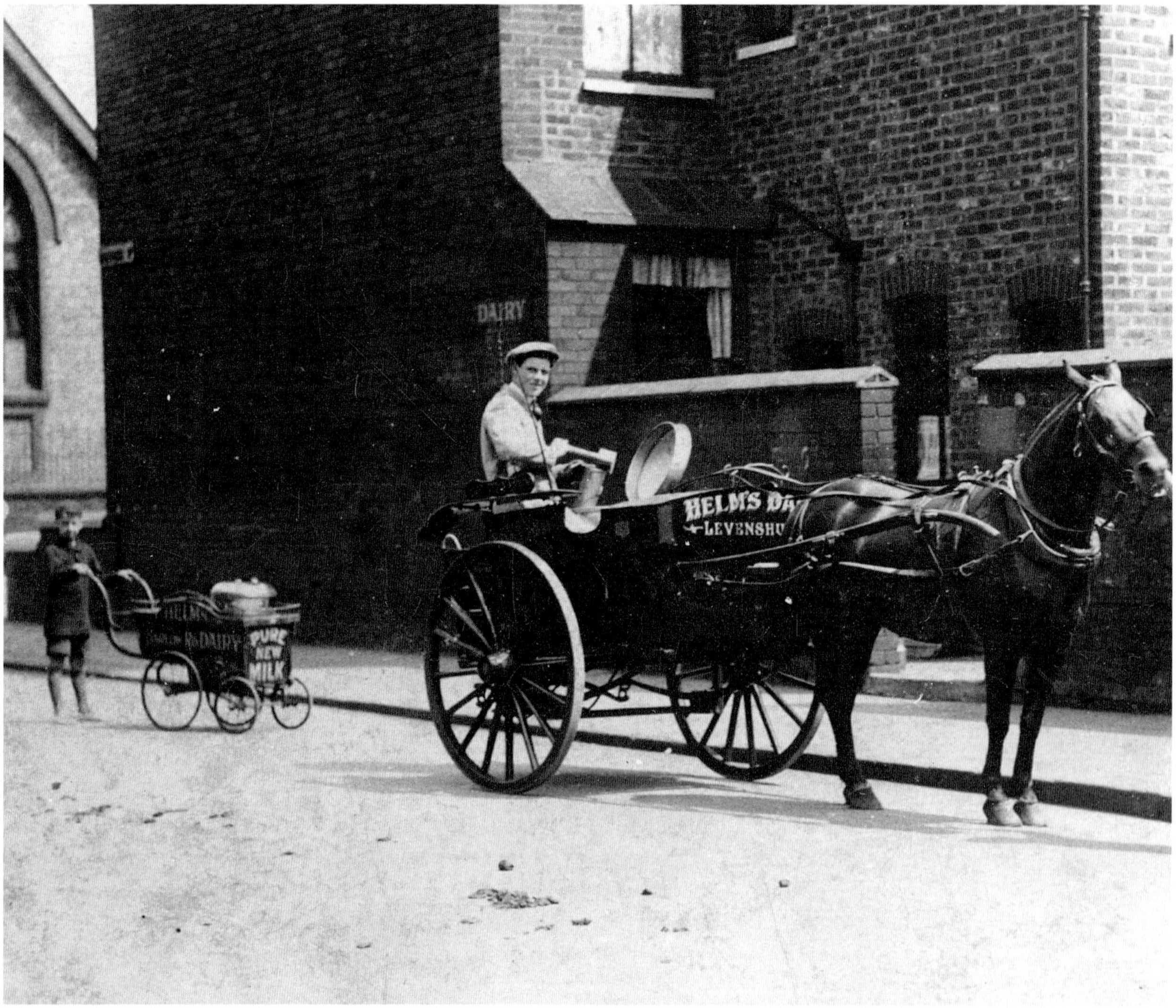

Helms Dairies in 1908, showing a horse-drawn cart and hand cart.

traffic all day long and most of the night. There are myriads of side streets leading to and from Stockport Road so that it is impossible to imagine the conditions of the turnpike road days when Stockport Road was not accessed for the length of Levenshulme by any other roads or lanes. The rows of neat terrace houses are now home to many Asian families who have moved to the area to work and study. The bright colours of their clothes and textiles, the temptingly spicy smells of their cuisine and the richness of their culture have brought a cosmopolitan flavour to Levenshulme. In the middle of all this Slade Hall survives in all its Tudor glory. It is tempting to wonder sometimes what the original Danish owner, Leofwine, would make of his 'island' now.

Further reading:
Sussex, Gay, Peter Helm and Andrew Brown *Looking back at Levenshulme and Burnage* Willow Publishing, 1987
Frangopulo, N.J. *Rich Inheritance* M/CR Education Committee, 1962

Longsight

Birch Lane in 1960. The BBC Television Studios, with an outdoor broadcast van just leaving.

There appears to be no immediate explanation for Longsight's name, save a legend that Bonnie Prince Charlie stopped there (as he seemed to do everywhere in Manchester) and one of his generals was heard to remark that 'it was a long sight to Manchester'. There is often a grain of truth in folklore but this tale does seem rather far-fetched, although Longsight is a comparatively modern name. A clue to an earlier definition of this area, which is sandwiched between Ardwick and Gorton, may lie in the name of Grindlow Marsh. Grindlow is of Saxon origin and means a green hill used as a burial mound. It is commemorated in the name of Grindlow Street by the police station. The present A6, known in Longsight as Stockport Road, follows the line of the old Roman road which led towards Buxton and runs straight through the middle of Longsight. This has long been an important route

Kirkmanshulme Lane in 1915. It was formerly part of Newton Heath.

Stanley Grove with overhead tramlines in 1925.

and it would have been dotted with small settlements. There was certainly a Grindlow Marsh Farm according to a map of 1844 (which shows most of the area regarded as present day Longsight as being in Gorton or Openshaw) and Longsight Hall stood opposite Grindlow Marsh. One of the original settlements along the old road could well have been Grindlow, which was exchanged at a later date for the more catchy and colloquial Longsight.

Longsight is bounded on the east by Hyde Road and on the west by Anson Road and Beresford Road. It was incorporated with Manchester in 1890. Belle Vue zoological gardens and a greyhound track lay in the western part of the suburb until the 1970s/1980s, while Victoria Park lies to the south-west where Longsight borders on Rusholme. The toll gates for the park used to be in Anson Road near the Daisy Bank Road corner. A large railway works complex occupies much of the northern sector while the southern sector is a jumble of small streets. Present-day Longsight is very much a creature of the Industrial Revolution, although its industry was limited because no canals or rivers run through the township. The most impressive works are the Longs-

Slade Hall, Slade Lane, on 18 May 1951. It was built in 1585 on Longsight border by George and Edward Siddall.

ight engine sheds and maintenance/engineering works, which today are used for the same purposes by Eurostar.

There were few textile manufactories in Longsight. The Longsight Silk Mill on Stockport Road was one of the foremost but sadly it was destroyed by fire in 1869. There was a cotton mill in Crowcroft Park which also borders on Levenshulme; the Co-op Print Works stood on Hamilton Road and Daisy Works Mill on Stockport Road. This mill was badly damaged by fire in 1928 but continued to operate until 1939 when it was taken over by the War Office and used as a pay office. After the war Daisy Bank did not re-open as a working mill. Corn Mill stood in New Bank Street and in Knutsford Vale there were iron works, bleachers and a clay pit for making bricks. Today Asian clothing manufacture is the main industry.

What makes Longsight remarkable is the extraordinary number of schools and churches within the township. There are seven primary schools, three secondary schools and one special needs school, Longsight School (built 1970) on Cochrane Avenue. The oldest primary school is St John's C of E School on Mitre Road, built in 1831. St Joseph's RC Junior School on Richmond Grove, run by the Brothers of the Christian Schools since 1871, is an amalgamation of two homes for working-class boys (over-16s from Grindlow Street and under-16s from Richmond Grove). St Joseph's also has a modern (1964) Infants School on Laindon Road and a High School for Girls on Upper Laindon Road. The Central High School for Boys has its lower school on Daisy Bank Road while the upper school is in Kirkmanshulme Road. It is worth noting that the former Longsight Grammar School was in Hayley Street next to the old Longsight Library. Other schools include St Agnes's C of E School (1835) in Clitheroe Road; St Clement's C of E School (1862) in Langport Avenue; St Robert's RC Junior School (1929) on Montgomery Road; and Plymouth Grove Primary School (1906) on Plymouth Grove West.

However, it is the number and diversity of the churches in Longsight, a suburb that hardly existed until 200 years ago, which is truly amazing, along with the fact that many have survived. St John's Church on St John's Road was the oldest church in Levenshulme, built in 1845–6, and was also the only church to have a graveyard, although burials ceased in 1966. In 1979 it was amalgamated with St Cyprian's Church on Plymouth Grove. The Calvinist Methodist Church in Daisy Bank Road was known as the 'Welsh Church' because it provided 'a spiritual home for Welsh exiles' from 1913–51. It is now Longsight Spiritualist Church. The College Chapel Methodist Church on Dickenson Road was only active from 1907–78, although there was a Sunday school there in 1893. Today it is the West Indian Church of the God of Prophecy. The architect, Edgar Wood, designed the Edgar Wood Centre in Daisy Bank Road. He was influenced by William Morris and the English Arts and Crafts movement. It was the First Church of Christ, Scientist, from 1903–78 and prompted Nikolaus Pevsner to write of it in his many-volume work on English architecture: 'the only religious building in Lancashire that would be indispensable in a survey of 20th-century church design in all England'. The building is now the drama and music department for Manchester College of Higher Education.

The Independent Chapel in Lime Grove (off Stockport Road), known as the Ivy Chapel because of the heavy growth of ivy on its front wall, was Longsight's most fashionable church between 1853 and 1933. Longsight Free Christian Church stood on the corner of Birch Lane and Plymouth Grove. It was also known as the Unitarian Chapel and had strong links with William Gaskell, a Unitarian minister who tutored Beatrix Potter's father, Rupert, and was the husband of the novelist Elizabeth Gaskell. A datestone with his name and the date 23 September 1882 stood upside-down in front of the church from 1887–1948. When it closed it was used by the BBC as a van depot and then became a warehouse. The Tin Tabernacle, Longsight's Baptist Church, started life in an iron building on the corner of Slade Grove and Slade Lane in 1887 and was rebuilt in 1898, while the Sunday school opened in 1929. Today it is known as the Church of God, Seventh Day Adventists. The Ukrainian Orthodox Church opened in 1974 in buildings on Plymouth Grove and 'the interior is full of light, flowers and brightly coloured portraits'. On Beresford Road stands the Reformed Church of Jesus Christ of the Latter Day Saints (Mormon church) which opened in 1923 after believers had spent some time having meetings in a room over a coal yard on Mundy Street.

Other churches include: Roby Congregational Church on Dickenson Road (built 1911); Longsight Methodist Church on Stockport Road (1853–1966, when a new church and community centre was built next door); Longsight Presbyterian Church on Stockport Road (1870–1962) which also had a Sunday school, and a church hall where the Longsight Players met; Northmoor Road (now North Road) Methodist Church (built 1911) which was a Wesleyan Methodist chapel with a school; St Agnes's Church on Hamilton Road (built 1885); St Clement's Church on Grey Street (built 1876 and now demolished); and St Robert's RC Church on Hamilton Road which opened in 1970.

In 1843 John Jennison expanded the Belle Vue Tea Gardens, established in 1836 on Hyde Road, by 13 acres and included a lake, a natural history museum and an entrance from the Longsight side. This was followed in 1847 by the addition of a maze to the gardens and the building of a greyhound track near the Longsight entrance. In 1850 a two-storey building was constructed at the Longsight entrance which housed a ballroom for 500 people. Over the next 50 years monkeys, camels, bears, lions, elephants and a sealion pool were added to the gardens, and the Italian Gardens, a new maze, the Indian Grotto and a fireworks stand were constructed. A larger ballroom was built for 10,000

Daisy Works Mill in 1932.

Birch Park in 1900, with its ornate fountain and bandstand.

people. The funfair, roller skating, a scenic railway and a miniature railway, speedway, stockcar racing, a 32-lane bowling alley, circuses and regular performances by the Halle Orchestra followed in the 20th century. By the 1970s, however, Belle Vue, though offering so much, had had its day, and the gates closed for the last time on 30 January 1982.

Today Longsight is a growing multicultural society. The population has risen to over 16,500, an increase of over 11 percent since 1991. There is a Pakistani community centre, the Darus Salam Islamic Centre, an Islamic law centre and a centre for refugees. Eastern influence can be seen in the food shops, the butchers that sell halal meat and in the beautiful Indian fabrics for sale in the textile stores. There is an Asian greengrocers in an old cinema. Stockport Road is a constant stream of heavy traffic and the heart of the suburb has an air of bustle about it. There is a modern library and a small shopping complex. Longsight is changing rapidly and ironically a new textile industry has begun to take root, run by hardworking Asian families. History, as they say, is cyclical.

Further reading:
Sussex, Gay *Longsight past and present*, 1982.

Miles Platting

Miles Platting is tucked away, a small unobtrusive suburb surrounded by Clayton, Ancoats and Newton Heath. For population counts and political purposes Miles Platting is included in a central ward with Ancoats and the city, but while Ancoats has its own strong identity as a distinct area, Miles Platting does not, although it is remembered with some affection by those who lived there. How or why or when the suburb came into being is uncertain. There is no mention of Miles Platting in early records and the origins of the name are not clear. Platt is a small piece of ground and miles can mean a mile or a mill. The name does appear on a map of 1820 and it is most likely that Miles Platting was born a child of the Industrial Revolution which so changed the face of Manchester.

Oldham Road and Hulme Hall Road bound Miles Platting. In late Victorian times Miles Platting was home to Hollands Mill, Victoria Mills and Ducie Mills; to Morgan and Crossleys; to Hardman and Holdens; to a chemical works, a timber yard and a forge; and, during the 1870s, to a tannery in the Providence Works. A gas works stood on Bradford Road, which also boasted 10 public houses. Ten public houses on one street speaks volumes about living conditions and lifestyles of the time. There were rows of streets full of back-to-back small terraced houses and there was a Ragged School on Charter Street. St Paul's Church lay on Oldham Road and St Mark's Church was built in 1900. St Mark's ran an active Boys Brigade. Life was harsh but there was a real sense of community and far less delinquency as a result of social problems than there would be just a century later.

Miles Platting railway station, now demolished, lay where the Lancashire and Yorkshire Railway swung through 90 degrees to run across extensive tank sidings. An eyewitness account survives of Queen Victoria's royal train passing through Miles Platting station on its return journey after the queen had opened the Manchester Ship Canal in 1894. The platform was packed with excited children smiling

Workers' cottages in 1898.

A general view showing redevelopment and regeneration in 1970.

Sandal Street at the junction with Stracey Street, 1901. A Miles Platting millscape.

The playing fields and playground on the site of Hulme Hall Recreation Ground in 1908. The density of mills is overwhelming.

and waving. Although the Queen acknowledged them she did not smile in return, whereupon one small boy remarked that he thought she looked a 'bit of a sauerkraut!', a tongue-in-cheek reference to her German origins. Perhaps the grimness of the millscapes depressed her but a smile would have cost her nothing in comparison to what it had cost Manchester to lay the foundations for the wealth of her Empire.

Some idea of the density of population in Miles Platting (although individual figures aren't known) can be gauged from the number of schools and churches. These included Miles Platting Mission on Oldham Road, St Mark's, St Paul's, Corpus Christi, St Barnabas's, St Luke's and the Albert Memorial. St Mark's and the Albert Memorial had schools attached and there were also Holland Street School, Nelson Street School and, later in the 20th century, Miles Platting Secondary School, Leacroft special school and Metcalf Street day nursery. There is no separate incorporation date for Miles Platting with Manchester and it was probably incorporated with the original borough in 1838 along with Beswick, Ardwick and Ancoats.

Today Miles Platting is part of the East Manchester Regeneration Scheme. There is a Community Renewal Scheme and a community school, the Nicholas Varley School on Nelson Street. Opposite Sawley Road is the Carrioca (East Manchester) Business Park. Nearby is a public house with the rather quaint name of Spanking Roger. Opposite the basilica of Corpus Christi is a sensory resource centre and next-door to the church there is a social club. Close by are a modern swimming pool and a new library, one of only three in Manchester where security does not seem to be a problem. Like Ancoats, Miles Platting is rejuvenating itself and may soon become rather more than a little backwater suburb.

Further reading:
Roberts, Fred *Memories of a Victorian childhood and working life in Miles Platting* Neil Richardson, 1986

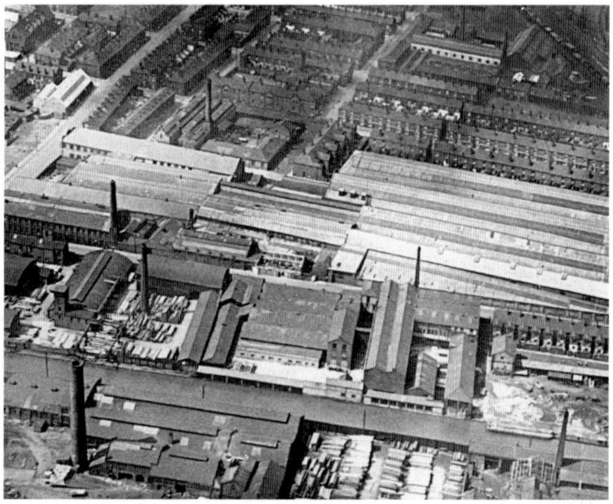

An aerial view of 1926, showing West's Gas Improvement Works and the John and William Bellhouse Ltd Timber Yard.

Moss Side

To look at Moss Side today is to find it almost impossible to imagine the quiet picturesque country village where Victorian ladies had their picnics in rich green meadows full of buttercups, as recently as the 1880s and 1890s. The thriving multicultural urban suburb of the 21st century is a completely different world. In the north of England a moss, as well as being a small flowerless plant, is a term often used to refer to a peat bog, taking its name from the sphagnum moss which grows in such places. Lindow Moss in nearby Cheshire is probably the best known moss because of the discovery of Lindow Man during the early 1980s. Moss Side, as the name suggests, lay on the edge of a moss which would have provided turf for building and fuel. Although the Domesday Book dismisses most of the south Manchester area as 'wasteland' (i.e. not cultivated or used for grazing), Moss Side has been an inhabited hamlet since early mediaeval times. Hamlet it certainly was. Even as late as 1801 the population only amounted to 150 people, most of whom made a living from agriculture. In her novel *Mary Barton* (published in 1848), Elizabeth Gaskell features Pepperhill Farm and describes the idyllic rural scenes in Moss Side and the pleasure gained by Manchester townspeople in visiting them.

However, the end of the 19th century and the beginning of the 20th century brought major changes to Moss Side. During the 40 years from 1861–1901 the population increased ten-fold to 27,000. Moss Side is laid out within a grid system (like Rusholme) due to modern planned evolution rather than to natural evolution over the centuries. The main roads are Princess Road, Alexandra Road, Moss Lane East and West, Great Western Street (which links Rusholme and Whalley Range), Graeme Street and Upper Lloyd Street. These are intersected by a number of shorter narrower streets. Building development began in earnest later in Moss Side than in some of the other suburbs such as Ardwick, Hulme and Chorlton, so the terraced houses tended to be of better quality because they were subject to

Moss Side farm in 1900. It was the last farm in Moss Side.

Moss Side Fire Brigade with fire engine in 1906.

Old cottages in 1884.

building regulations. Some even had tiny front gardens which were much prized as status symbols.

Greenheys in the Denmark Road area of Moss Side boasted larger, solidly built middle-class homes. Residents included Sir Charles Halle, who gave his name to the Halle Orchestra; and Rupert Potter, father of the internationally acclaimed children's writer, Beatrix Potter, was born at 208 Exmouth Road in 1833. The gentility of large parts of Moss Side was accentuated by fine buildings like the Denmark Hotel on Lloyd Street and the creation of Alexandra Park. It is an indication of the growth period of Moss Side that several features were named after Princess Alexandra of Denmark, who became the queen of Victoria's eldest son, Edward VII. The park was opened in 1876. Facilities included two miles of walking paths, two and a half miles of carriage drives, a large lake used for boating in summer and skating in winter, a pavilion and a bandstand. Sunday afternoon concerts of light classical music were popular. Ladies promenaded in floaty dresses, shading themselves with parasols, and bored children found ways in which to amuse themselves while their parents listened to the music.

In 1894 Moss Side acquired an Urban District Council which undertook public works such as the building of council offices on Moss Lane East, a fire station, and Moss Side public library, which opened in 1896 adjacent to the council offices. Previously, library facilities had been provided through outlets like Harpers Circulating Library, which stood on the corner of Denmark Road and Monton Street. Essential services, however, such as water, gas and sewerage, were provided by Manchester, into which Moss Side was incorporated in 1904 despite much local opposition. The tram depot on Princess Road was built in 1909 and was later enlarged to accommodate 300 trams. By the 1930s buses had taken the place of trams but the depot is still in use today by Stagecoach bus services in conjunction with their depot on Hyde Road in Ardwick.

Pepperhill Farm (demolished 1900) in 1870. This was Mary Barton's farm in the novel Mary Barton *by Elizabeth Gaskell.*

Cecil Street (Nos 63–65), which were rented by Friedrich Engels during the 1840s. They became the Commercial Hotel in 1866–8.

A number of churches were built to cater for the rapidly growing population. St James's Church on Princess Road; Christ Church on Upper Lloyd Street; and a trio of churches on Moss Lane East,

A steam wagon has crashed into a lamp-post at the junction of Princess Road and Moss Lane East in 1906.

Terraced housing on Cowesby Street in 1968.

including the Church of the New Age, the Swedenborgian Church, and, on the corner with Raby Street, the Raby Street Wesleyan Methodist Church. The Polish Church of Divine Mercy was built in the late 1960s. Although schools were often attached to or associated with the churches, Moss Side School Board built a large Board School on Princess Road in 1896. On the first day 800 children turned up to enrol. Later there were a number of primary schools built, including Greenheys County Primary and Moss Side Primary near Whitworth Park. Secondary schools included the Loreto Convent and Ducie High School.

Maine Road is home to 'the Blues' of Manchester City Football Club, whose fortunes in recent years have been mixed. Manchester City was the name chosen by Ardwick Football Club in 1894, two years after becoming a member of the Football League's Second Division. Ardwick Football Club was itself an amalgamation of West Gorton St Mark's (founded in 1880) and Gorton Athletic (formed in 1884). Their original ground was in Ardwick near the Hyde Road bus depot, but they moved to Maine Road in 1923.

The population has declined by over 10 percent

Mees Farm, Whalley Farm, off Withington Road, Alexandra Park, in 1897.

Alexandra Park in 1910. The park was named after the queen of Edward VII.

in the last 10 years and is now around 11,700. There is a new learning centre in Greenheys and the Powerhouse has been set up to help disaffected and disadvantaged young people. Sadly, however, modern pressures and developments have meant that Moss Side has lost its sense of community and identity and there have been savage social problems which have led to Moss Side earning Manchester the nickname of 'Gunchester', something that would have been totally unimaginable to the Victorian ladies who took their children there to enjoy the tranquillity and picnic by the river and play in the meadows.

In the first four months of 2002, 19 shooting incidents took place in Moss Side and neighbouring Longsight, and in May 2002 armed police began regular street patrols in both suburbs. It is a world removed from the rural peace of Pepperhill Farm.

Further reading:
Makepeace, Chris *Looking back at Hulme, Moss Side, Chorlton on Medlock and Ardwick* Willow Publishing, 1998
Crofton, Henry Thomas *Old Moss Side* Manchester City Council, 1903

The Central Establishment Laundry showing a four roller callender in 1935.

Moston

'The knight he rode east, t'wards the uprising sun
but the broad heaths of Moston lay silent and dun.'

These lines are taken from *The Wild Rider of Lancashire* by Samuel Bamford and describe a Moston that is now unrecognisable. Samuel Bamford was a mill worker who spent the last 14 years of his life living in Hall Street in Moston, where his neighbour was the Failsworth-born dialect poet and playwright, Ben Brierley. Bamford was also a poet, a journalist and a social reformer, and he was involved at Peterloo in 1819. He was one of several speakers who addressed an 80,000 strong crowd in St Peter's Fields, calling for 'reforms to conditions which condemned thousands to a life of poverty, wretchedness, tyranny and injustice,' the unacceptable price which ordinary working people were paying for the Industrial Revolution. The authorities panicked and called in the troops, who opened fire after failing to seize revolutionary banners. They then rode into the crowd on their horses and slashed mercilessly and indiscriminately with their sabres. Eleven people died and 500 were injured, many seriously. The Peterloo Massacre has gone down in history as a totally unjustified and violent repression of peaceful unarmed civilians. The folk memory was so strong that even a century and a half after the event there was still hesitation in allowing mounted police to patrol the streets of Manchester. Samuel Bamford was arrested after Peterloo and sentenced to a year's imprisonment for 'conspiracy to alter the legal frame of government... and meeting tumultuously at Manchester...'

Moston is first mentioned in around 1100. The name means simply a village by the moss or lake; or even a marshy farmstead. Moston may have originated as the latter in Anglo-Saxon times and grown to a village by 1100. The moss from which the township took its name may well have been White Moss, about a mile from Moston Hall. Moston, like neighbouring Blackley, lies on the northern edge of the Manchester suburbs, well away

Mrs Fox's Toffee Shop, formerly the toll bar, at the corner of Nuthurst Road with Moston Lane in 1905.

The Chain Bar toll house on Moston Lane in 1890.

from the city, and bordered on heath, moss and moorland. This saved the township from the worst ravages of the Industrial Revolution. In 1854, Revd John Booker wrote in his work *A History of the Ancient Chapel of Blackley* that '... Moston enjoyed a reputation unequalled by all the other suburbs of Manchester, as the residence of families of distinction...' Nearly 60 years later, in 1911, Moston was still being written about in romantic nostalgic terms. 'The smell of the hawthorn in spring, and of the grass and the hay in summer, and of the fading leaves in autumn, and the smell of burnt wood or peat in winter... the windswept fields of Moston carried quite as much vitality in them...' (John Wood. *Moston Characters at Work*, 1911).

The names of Moston certainly had a delightfully wild ring to them. White Moss, Nuthurst, Theile Moor, (or Theyle Moor: there is a brief reference to Theyle Cross in 1595 and a boundary dispute over grazing rights in the 1520s) with plenty of cloughs and wastes. In 1907 H.T. Crofton described the Moston topography as follows:

> ... from Moston Brook four cloughs or ravines run north... one on the west called Harpurhey Clough (running upwards from Moston Bottoms), one midway called Dean Clough, and further east there are two close together, of which the westerly is called Boar Green Clough and leads to Great Nuthurst Hall, and to the east of the last mentioned Clough, Moston Brook is called Morris Brook in Morris Clough.

Harpurhey Clough has disappeared under an urban sprawl. Dean Clough, where Moston Hall lay, is now part of Broadhurst Park, while Boar Green Clough disappeared under Moston Pit Colliery and the railway.

In the 13th century however, the scene looked rather different. The Moston family lived at Moston

Moss House Farm, 1937.

Moston Bottoms in 1920. The boy is standing on the site of the Coffin Well.

Hall in Dean Clough (or Kitchen Clough as it was also called); the Chetham's lived in Great Nuthurst Hall, to which Boar Green Clough led (the site today lies on the west side of the railway between Glanton Walk and Enstone Drive on the Mill Estate); and the Chaddertons (formerly called the de Trafford family) lived at Little Nuthurst Hall (between Nuthurst Road, Oakwood Avenue and Greenways). On old title deeds 148 Nuthurst Road is called Little Nuthurst Farm. The Chetham's were the lords of the manor since both the Mostons and Chaddertons paid rent to them, and the Chetham family remained at Great Nuthurst Hall for 650 years. Their estate was finally broken up in 1851 and 57 acres of that estate became what is now known as New Moston. By 1900 both Nuthurst Halls were in ruins. Moston Hall did not survive either; all that remained was a grassy mound which lay behind the Alexian Brothers Home. Moston Hall Farm survived until the 1870s. It is surmised that the original 12th-century Moston Hall, built by Ralph de Moston, was protected by an oak 'ring fence', a sort of fortified manor house. Moston Hall was said to be haunted but by whom remains a mystery.

Lightbowne Hall stood on Kenyon Lane near the junction with Lightbowne Road. At first it was the home of the Jepson family, before passing by marriage to the Lightbownes in 1646. It was demolished in 1965, having been rectory to St Luke's Church since the church was built in 1910. The stone horse-mounting steps from the hall were taken to the churchyard of St Mary's (built in 1869). Hough Hall stood on Hough Hall Road behind Moston Lane School (one of three Board Schools; the others being in Lily Lane and New Moston). The hall was a Tudor farmhouse, built by the Asshetons of Middleton and sold to the Hough family in 1613. The Houghs were staunch Royalist supporters so during the Civil War the hall was temporarily confiscated. The hall was then sold to James Lightbowne, and after passing through marriage to first the Minshull family and then the Aytoun family, it was sold to Samuel Taylor. He built Moston House in 1776 on the site of the present Margaret Ashton Sixth Form College. The college was formerly Harpurhey High School for Girls, which in 1886 was taken over by the Daughters of the Cross (a religious house from Liège) to establish a home for

The Nuthurst Road bridge over the Lancashire and Yorkshire Railway, 1900.

Shackliffe Green, the cottage known as Atkinson (demolished May 1908), on 17 November 1907.

30 orphan girls and to provide accommodation for those Daughters teaching at Mount Carmel school.

According to the *Survey of the Manor of Manchester* in 1322 the tenants and burgesses of Moston and Nuthurst were to use '...the mill of Mamcestre running by the water of Irke... to grind their grain...' In 1547 the Bowker family owned a part of Moston. Bowker comes from 'bowking', which is the washing and bleaching of linen (then done on the banks of rivers or streams). Moston inhabitants were earning a living from making white linen yarn as early as 1595. Fustian is a tough fabric, a mixture of linen and cotton, and fustian cutters worked from a row of old cottages on Moston Lane. A wadding mill was built in 1714, the first recorded mill in Moston. The Street family, good yeoman farming stock, lived at Street Fold and gave their name to the place. Moston was after all essentially a farming community and the Moston Farmers Rent Dinner was still being held as late as the 1850s. However, like neighbouring Harpurhey, Moston specialised in the dyeing and bleaching processes and by 1820 Moston Print and dye works stood near the junction of William's Road and St Mary's Road. This was followed shortly afterwards by Dean Brook dye works, which was built near the convergence of Dean Brook and Moston Brook. Part of the site lay in Newton Heath which borders Moston, and a proportion of the rates had to be paid to Newton Heath. This mill, however, had disappeared by 1911. Moston Mill, a cotton-spinning mill, was built in 1910. The Industrial Revolution seemed to have finally taken hold but just 40 years later, Moston turned the tables. The first digital computer system in the world, which would herald a new technological revolution, was built in Moston and unveiled by Manchester University in July 1951.

Street Fold on 2 June 1937, showing the Simpson Memorial Building on the left, which today houses Moston Library.

Moston also had a colliery. There had been opencast mining in the area since Tudor times from seams under White Moss and Theyle Moor. The first shaft of Moston Pit was sunk to a depth of 1,000ft (about 330m) in 1840 near Nuthurst Railway Bridge and the second shaft was sunk 10 years later to almost the same depth in the Kop-thorne near Moston Mill. The colliery was leased in 1874 by

Hough Hall in 1895. The hall was built by the Assheton family in Tudor times.

Platt Brothers, who were textile machinery manufacturers, the Railway Steel and Plant Company, and the Broughton Cooper Company. Flooding was always a problem and led to the abandonment of shafts one and two in 1886. Four hundred people were thrown out of work causing great distress. The third shaft was sunk in 1884 just to the south of the first shaft. This was the deepest shaft at a depth of 586 yards (around 550m) but the 'crushed strata of Moston Fault' led to problems when working the coal seams. The fourth and final shaft, and the shallowest at 205 yards (around 200m) deep, was sunk in 1887 about 30 yards away from the third shaft. The last two shafts lay in a square bounded by Bradford Court, Moston Court, Woodstock Road and Teddington Road. On the morning of 11 March 1940 there was a serious accident when seven trucks derailed and crashed to the bottom of No.17 slant, killing six miners and injuring 15. Moston Colliery finally closed on 5 June 1950. An estate for workers from the Bradford Colliery was built on the site.

Moston suffered from severe population increase like all the other suburbs. In the half-century prior to 1831 the population had increased by just 52 people. In the half-century following 1831 the population increased by over 10,000 people. Today the population stands at around 12,500; a decline of 2 percent on 1991. The increase in the population brought with it a building boom and a rash of new churches and schools. There were a number of Methodist churches plus St Dunstan's, St John's, St Mary's and St George's Churches. St Mary's and St Dunstan's had schools attached and a number of

Moston Toll Bar, on the corner of St Mary's Road and Nuthurst Road, in 1892.

other schools were built including a Board School built in 1899, a number of primary schools and the North Manchester Grammar School for Boys. Moston was incorporated with Manchester in 1890, based mainly on a need, like every other Manchester suburb, for assistance with sanitary administration and the problems of sewage and its disposal. The City Council was only too happy to take over the expense and management of these facilities in return for further expansion and development, and rehousing people from slum clearance areas in Manchester from the 1880s onwards.

Today there is little trace of ancient Moston left. MANCAT has a campus on Moston Lane for further and adult education. A decent library and museum are housed in the Simpson Memorial Institute, built in 1888 on Moston Lane through endowment from the estate of a local handloom silk weaver, William Simpson. There is an industrial estate on Tulketh Street. The Board School survives as Moston Lane Community Primary School. St Dunstan's Church and Holy Trinity Primary School have also survived. The area now known as Moston Village is quite pleasant and is home to the Drawing Room restaurant, a name evocative of a bygone age. Moston also has a famous 20th-century son, the well-known television historian Michael Wood, whose searches for the past, both in his own country and abroad, have fascinated millions of people. A fitting tribute for this particular suburb, which has undergone such a complete transformation in the last 150 years.

Further reading:
Searle, Father Brian *Moston Story*, 1983

Newton Heath

The suburb of Newton Heath in Manchester is known locally as Newton. However, about eight miles away is another settlement called Newton which forms part of Tameside in Greater Manchester, so the name Newton Heath will not be abbreviated here in order to avoid confusion or mistakes. Newton Heath takes its name from the Old English for 'the new village on the heath', although it is difficult to assess where the original settlement might have lain. In former times the heath stretched from Miles Platting to Failsworth. What is now Oldham Road ran part of the way across. The heath lay on the route that connected the Roman forts of Castlefield (in central Manchester) and Castleshaw (near Oldham). In 1856 excavations in Gaskell Street revealed a

Manchester Floorcloth Works in William Street on 13 November 1895.

The Chinese bazaar at All Saints' Sunday school in 1899.

Today Newton Heath is bounded by Failsworth, the River Medlock, Shooters Brook, Newton Brook and Moston Brook. In addition there is an area of land, formerly known as Newton Detached, and more recently as Kirkmanshulme, which is also part of Newton Heath. Belle Vue stood on this land, although access to Belle Vue was from Hyde Road in Ardwick and Stockport Road in Longsight. Close to where the River Medlock flows under Clayton Bridge a corn mill stood at Millhouses from the 14th–19th century. In 1757 a mob rioted and attacked the mill because

Roman roadway which had been built on a base of logs so that it would not sink into the squelchy ground of the heath.

There were four gateways to the heath. Culcheth Gate (near Culcheth Gates Inn); Cheetham's Gate (on Briscoe Lane near the school); Dean's Gate (on the site of Dean Brook Inn); and Greaves' Gate (at the junction of Droylsden Road and Terrance Street). The heath was remote and largely uninhabited prior to the Industrial Revolution. Farming was the main livelihood and the small population of the area lived around four village greens: Goose Green (off Dean Lane); Hobson's Green (near Dob Lane Chapel); Botany Green (near Greaves' Gate); and Crown Point Green (off Briscoe Lane). The greens themselves were meeting places where the social life of the community took place. There was bull, bear and badger baiting; 'shinty', a game played with a ball, curved sticks and rugby-style goal posts, and dancing around the maypole on May Day. The maypole on Crown Point Green was topped by 'a crown presented by the Greaves family in 1746 after the Battle of Culloden as proof of loyalty to the House of Hanover'.

No.5 Great Newton Street, demolished by a falling mill chimney, 13 January 1899. Ten people lived there and several of them died.

The Droylsden Road bridge over the Rochdale Canal, 1905.

of rumours that the miller was adding ground human bones to his flour.

Johnson's map of Manchester, drawn in 1820, shows large parts of Newton Heath as uninhabited. Culcheth Hall, which stood on a bend of the River Medlock in Clayton Vale (at the edge of the Newton Heath township) was initially owned by the Byrons of Clayton Hall and later by a prominent Lancashire family, the Greaveses, whose name is still commemorated within the district. Whitworth Hall, built in 1639 and one of the oldest brick houses in Manchester, stood where the railway crosses Queens Road. Hulme Hall lay nearby on what is now Hulme Hall Lane. Monsall House, just north of the Whitworth Hall, formed part of the Monsall Estate. Today, Monsall Hospital, a children's and isolation hospital, stands on the site. Oldham Road, running diagonally from west to east across the township, was turnpiked in the 18th century and the toll bar was at the junction with Lamb Lane. The Rochdale Canal, built in 1804, follows the line of the road closely but a little to the south. The only churches shown in the parish in 1820 are All Saints' on Graver Lane and Dob Lane Dissenting Chapel.

The building of the Rochdale Canal sealed the fate of Newton Heath. In 1801 the population was 1,291 and it was still essentially a farming community full of ancient traditions such as 'a-Maying'; rushbearing in August (the old Celtic festival of Lughnasa) when a cart of fantastically piled heaps of rushes garlanded with flowers would be dragged to the local church for the rushes to be strewn on the cold stone floors; and a strong belief in the power of witchcraft. Even during the latter half of the 20th century the logo of a witch in a pointed hat and riding on her broomstick was used for Newton Heath Traction Maintenance depot.

Thirty years later the population had risen to 6,127 (almost a five-fold increase) and by 1871 it was 18,079. There had been a cottage industry of linen weaving and bleaching along the banks of the Medlock since 16th-century French Huegenot refugees had settled in the area. Linen was laid out to dry in the fields after bleaching and anyone caught stealing could expect the worst. As late as 1798 a local lad was publicly executed in Newton Heath for 'stealing from a bleaching croft'. The coming of the mills changed all that. In 1825 Newton Silk Mill and Monsall Silk dye works collaborated in the production of sarsnet, a soft silk fabric used for ribbons. Cotton-spinning and silk/cotton/linen weaving mills sprang up along the banks of the Medlock and the Rochdale Canal. So too did Sankey's Soap Works, Cardwell's Rope Works, engineering and glass manufacturing works and even a factory which made matches. Farming collapsed as people flocked to the area to work in the mills and factories. 'Scores of small cheap terraced houses were built to accommodate them', particularly around the Oldham Road area.

During the 1840s another major innovation, which was to have long-lasting effects, took place. The Lancashire and Yorkshire Railway built two main lines across the area, both of which ran from Manchester via neighbouring Miles Platting to Yorkshire. Engine repair sheds and carriage works, under the grand name of Newton Heath Traction Maintenance Depot, were built in 1877. There were 24 'roads' (i.e. parallel lines) for locomotives which required work done on them. By 1932 the depot employed over 1,000 staff. Shortly after the railway had opened a young woman was killed in an accident on thc line. Her body was taken to the local mortuary, which was in the old stables of the 18th-century Duke of York hotel. Afterwards, unexplained footsteps were often heard in the bar and downstairs rooms. The footsteps continued to be heard for well over a century until one dark windswept night during the 1960s the stable roof collapsed. Nothing more was heard after that and ironically a health centre now stands on the spot where the crushed and lifeless body of the young woman once lay awaiting burial. In 1886 the Lancashire and Yorkshire Railway moved its carriage works from Horwich to Newton Heath. Carriages, goods wagons and lorries were built on the 40-acre site and about 2,000 people were employed. There was a staff canteen on Thorpe Road where employees could take their own food to be cooked for their lunch by the serving staff. The works closed down in 1932.

In 1878 a football team was formed from the

The All Saints' Whit Walk in 1905.

The Farmyard Tavern (formerly a working farm) on Ten Acres Lane at Baguley Fold on 28 March 1907. The inn was disused by 1917.

Lancashire and Yorkshire Railways employees who worked at Newton Heath Traction Maintenance Depot. They played at the North Road pitch on Monsall Road. It was a successful team which became known as the Heathens, partly a corruption of the name Newton Heath and partly because the Traction Maintenance Depot logo was a witch. After gaining admission to the Football League in 1892 the North Road pitch proved to be unsuitable for games, because of the larger audiences, and the club moved to Bank Street in Clayton. In 1902 Newton Heath FC was re-christened Manchester United.

Newton Heath became a home for engineering works. The engineering firm of Heenan and Froude on Monsall Road was responsible for the building of Blackpool Tower, which took four years and opened in 1894. Tootal, best known for the manufacture of men's shirts, began life in 1799 on Ten Acres Lane when it was known as Tootal Broadhurst. Mather and Platt were founded in 1852 in Salford but moved to Park Works on Briscoe Lane in 1900. In 1881 the firm purchased the dynamo manufacturing rights from Thomas Edison. Following the move to Newton Heath the firm bought the Machinery Annexe from the Paris Exhibition of 1900 and shipped it to Park Works where it was reassembled as their machine shop. During World War One Mather and Platt worked with the firm of A.V. Roe on AVRO 504 aeroplane manufacture. After the war A.V. Roe built a factory on Ten Acres Lane. A.V. Roe continued to manufacture AVRO 504 planes and bodywork for Crossley Motors, while Mather and Platt became best known for their sprinkler systems.

Despite all this industry some farms survived in Newton Heath. These included Baguley Fold Farm, an infilled timbered building which was still a working farm in 1907 and two or three other farms on Ten Acres Lane; and the Farmyard Tavern, a farm which became an inn in 1900 selling ale brewed in Newton Heath. By 1917 there was only one working farm left and the Farmyard Tavern had fallen into disuse. The old country customs of May Day festivities, rushcart ceremonies, a belief in witchcraft and Whit Walks survived until after World War One.

The latter half of the 20th century finally saw the death of these ancient traditions. The decline in church attendance was partly responsible coupled with a youth culture which was more brash and streetwise than its predecessors and had a desire to dismiss the beliefs of yesteryear as old-fashioned rubbish. Several churches were demolished during the 1970s including St Ann's; St Augustine's (built 1888, closed 1967, destroyed by fire 1970); and St Cuthbert's (built 1889). One success story, however, was that of Christ the King Church, founded in response to the building of a corporation housing estate in the 1920s. The first mass was said on

Tootal Mens Wear (English Sewing Ltd) on Bower Street, 1982.

Christmas Day 1937 in the Convent Chapel of The Little Sisters of the Poor (an order founded in France in 1640 and dedicated to caring for the elderly). Christ the King School opened in 1939 and the church moved from a disused mill on Culcheth Lane to the school hall. A proper church was finally built in 1958, opened in 1960 and was consecrated in 1975.

A partner in the silk mill on Oldham Road, James Taylor, was a member of the family who owned Brookdale Hall. After his death, his son John inherited the hall and when he died in 1904 the estate was bought by Manchester Corporation and opened to the public as Brookdale Park. Newton Heath had been incorporated with Manchester in 1890. Brookdale Park gave its name to a new school which superseded the 'Tin School' (The Culcheth British School to give it its full ponderous title) on Regent Street. The Tin School was built from corrugated iron adjoining Culcheth Methodist Sunday School and had been running since 1869. In February 1931 the Tin School was transformed into school kitchens, cooking the school dinners for children attending Brookdale Park School. An even earlier school was All Saints' School, built adjoining All Saints' Church in the late 1680s. In 1772 the school was rebuilt outside the church grounds and enlarged in 1821. The Sunday school was separated in 1835. Rents from Todd's Charity helped to run the Sunday school. Todd's Charity was a row of cottages built in 1826 on the corner of All Saints' Street by Thomas Todd, a partner in the Culcheth Bleach Works. All Saints' School was then rebuilt on All Saints' Street in 1854 and again in 1961 on the site of the former All Saints' Rectory.

One of Manchester's leading suffragettes, Hannah Mitchell, had her home on Ingham Street. She was born in Derbyshire but moved to Bolton where she married Gibbon Mitchell, a fellow Socialist. She joined the Women's Suffrage Movement, working with the Pankhursts. She was briefly imprisoned in Strangeways and after this she moved to Newton Heath. She won a seat on Manchester City Council in 1924 and represented Newton Heath for a number of years. One of her main contributions was facilitating the building of a public washhouse on Worksleigh Street. She died in Newton Heath in 1956.

Today the population of Newton Heath is around 12,500 and the industrial area around the canal is run down. The terraced houses have been joined by modern blocks of flats. All Saints' Church and Christ the King School have survived, but the chapel on Culcheth Lane is now home to a car hire firm and the Culcheth Gates Inn is boarded up. Old Church Street is a thriving shopping centre, but the local library needs to be protected by high security measures. There is an astroturf sports complex on Ten Acres Lane. However, a tiny bit of the past still peeps through the curtains of time. Around Joyce Street a number of well-used allotments still flourish and one is used to house a flock of geese, ducks and chickens which enjoy going on walkabouts from time to time. They are a touching reminder of the farms and folds clustered around the wild uninhabited heathland of less than 200 years ago.

Further reading:
Newton Heath Historical Society *Looking Back at Newton Heath*, 1993.

Northenden

Sharston School in 1888. It had become the Sharston Tea Rooms by 1895 and was near the site of the Sharston Hotel.

Northenden was originally part of Cheshire, which is probably how it came to get its name 'northern dale or valley'. The River Mersey used to be the boundary and Northenden, lying just south of the river, would have been in the extreme north of Cheshire. It is an Anglo-Saxon name which translates literally as 'clearing of the north'. Northenden is recorded in the Domesday Book thus:

> ... in Bucklow Hundred – Randle and Bigot hold of the Earl Norwordine. Ulvert held it as one manor and was a freeman. There is one hide (measure of land) that pays geld (gold). There is land for two ploughs. It is waste (lying fallow/not used). There is a church and two furlongs of woodland. It is worth three shillings. It was worth ten shillings in the reign of Edward the Confessor.

Clear written evidence that the Norman Conquest had caused something of a depression in farming. A church is mentioned and could have been St Wilfrid's Church, built on a small hill, (although not the present building) which was probably founded by Wilfrid, Bishop of Ripon, during the ninth century.

The church was rebuilt sometime in the 15th century. During the Civil War it was attacked by Roundhead troops and the east window smashed in 'a purge of idolatry'. It was believed that Catholics worshipped there although Catholicism had been outlawed since the Catholic Queen Mary (Tudor) had died almost a century earlier. The rector fled and took refuge in the ferry house down by the river. Henry Dunster then became the minister during Cromwell's Commonwealth period (1649–60). The church survived, however, and a rectory was built sometime during the 18th century. In 1840 a Church Infants School was added. The church itself was rebuilt in 1873 by Joseph Crowther, the architect who restored Manchester Cathedral. He retained the 15th-century tower, an ancient screen and an early font, and a rather unusual sundial with a base like a fluted bowl. The tower was restored in 1926 when it was noted that the earliest grave in the churchyard was dated 1596. The rectory and the church are both listed buildings, as is nearby Northen House, once owned by Lord Egerton.

For centuries Northenden was a small farming village lying on an ancient salters' way and at a convenient crossing point of the Mersey. There are

Queen Victoria's Diamond Jubilee celebrations in 1897.

records of a 'selion' (a strip of land) being granted to 'William the miller' in 1311 close to the weir on the river. It was a corn mill where the local people used to grind their corn, leaving some behind as payment for the miller. By the 1300s the mill had come under the control of the Tatton family at Wythenshawe Hall. The Tattons insisted that all their tenants should use it and pay dues to the Tatton coffers for the privilege. Both the mill and the weir were demolished during the early 1960s. Two mediaeval 'crook construction' cottages (where the wooden support beams are in the shape of a huge wooden 'A') stood opposite the Spread Eagle on Royle Green Road (which may have been part of the 13th-century Ryle Thorn Inn, owned and possibly built by Sir William de Baggiley of Baggiley Hall in Wythenshawe). The cottages became listed buildings in 1982 but were demolished the following day! Remnants of mediaeval strip farming, visible parallel to the river in the area of Swineworth, were still in use as allotments during the late 20th century; and on Lampits Lane there are traces of the former village pond. At the point where Lampits Lane joins the river there used to be a boathouse, a fair, and, in later centuries, a stadium that was used for roller-skating, boxing and concerts.

Ford Lane, which leads past the church and rectory to the river and the ford, follows the route of the old saltway. In mediaeval times crannocks of salt would be taken by packhorse from the Cheshire wiches (Nantwich, Northwich) through Northenden and Manchester across to the Yorkshire ports via the Longdendale Valley which lies on the Derbyshire/Yorkshire/Cheshire border. Ford Lane was also said to have been used by Bonnie Prince Charlie and his troops on their epic march south in 1745 to attempt to take the English crown. Most of the suburbs can claim some link with Bonnie Prince Charlie and Northenden is no exception. Rose Cottages, black and white timbered cottages built in 1701 on Church Road, would have witnessed his passing through. The cottages were demolished in the 1960s, being replaced by a caravan library before the permanent library was built in 1982.

Northenden remained a close-knit rural community until the late 19th century, escaping the creeping tentacles of the Industrial Revolution, although the cottage industry of spinning flax suffered a marked decline. Farming life continued as it always had. Cedars Farm on Church Road survived until the early 20th century before becoming Bunts Dairy. Horses were shod in the local smithy. The last

A working forge in 1900.

smithy, Moor End Forge on Longley Lane, was not demolished until the 1970s. Stressed city types found tranquillity in the quiet pretty countryside and an early tourist industry sprang up. There was an abundance of shops, teahouses and restaurants in the village and golfing facilities were available for those who wished to play. The French owner of one café on Palatine Road provided orchestras, entertainers and silent Charlie Chaplin films for his patrons.

Royle Green Road. The funeral of Mr Dyson of Bradley Gate House in 1902. He was murdered by his ex-butler.

A turning by the church on Ford Lane (Boat Lane) led to the river and to the ferry. The ferry, known as Jackson's Boat, was worked by ropes until a footbridge was built over the Mersey in the 1870s. The Boathouse Inn changed its name to the Tatton Arms in 1875. In 1901 Simon's Bridge was built by Lord Simon's father. The river was at its shallowest here between Didsbury and Northenden and the lane which ran across the bridge linked Northenden and Didsbury parish churches. There were four other public houses within 200 metres of Northenden church: the Spread Eagle, the Jolly Carter, the Church Inn (with the Oddfellows hall opposite) and the Crown (the oldest and smallest, often called the Corner Pin). On the village green, in front of the Church Inn, there had been a maypole and bear baiting and stalls of local pottery for sale, but these gave way to travelling fairs and entertainers as the 19th century wore on. The village centre shifted from around St Wilfrid's and focussed on the Church Road/Palatine Road/Kenworthy Lane junction sometime in the 1860s. Village education was catered for by St Wilfrid's Church of England School (built 1901) and the Methodist School (also built in 1901) on Victoria Road next to the 9m square Methodist Chapel built in 1812.

Lingard Road, 1904.

Tranquil as its setting was, Northenden was not without drama. In 1902 a murder took place with an unusual and unsavoury aftermath. A gentleman named John Dyson lived at Bradley Gate on Langley Lane, opposite the present Royle Green garage. He had a butler named Cotterill. What passed between the two men is not known, but Cotterill left Mr Dyson's employment feeling aggrieved. He later returned and shot Mr Dyson dead. He was cornered in a stable behind the Church Inn and the police were called. A gun battle ensued, during the course

of which Cotterill was killed himself. The Boer War was barely over and Cotterill was believed to have been pro-Boer, gaining him the nickname of Kruger in the locality. Mr Dyson had been a popular resident of Northenden and the mood of the crowd who had gathered to watch turned ugly. Elbowing the police aside they dragged Cotterill's body out of the barn and kicked it along the road like a football, hurling abuse as they went. When the police finally retrieved Cotterill's remains they were buried quickly and quietly in an unmarked grave in Northenden churchyard so as not to excite further reprisals.

Northenden was also able to boast some local notables among its population. Ravenswood on Church Road was the home of Joseph Johnson, who, together with the orator Henry Hunt, bore much of the responsibility for the gathering which resulted in the Peterloo Massacre of 1819. Local historian Arthur Royle, whose collection of books about Northenden is held in Wythenshawe Library, became manager of the District Bank when it opened in 1930 on Church Road. Sir Edward Watkin, the railway magnate, lived at Rose Hill, and had an enormous 'shar stone' brought to his gardens by horse and cart. Rose Hill subsequently became a children's hospital and then a remand home. Another large house, Beech House on Yew Tree Lane, was used as a hospital during World War One and later as a centre for clinic and district nurses. In 1935 an archway from Manchester Cathedral was placed temporarily in the grounds during restoration work on the cathedral.

The village of Northenden retained its rural charm into the 20th century. Kenworthy Lane and Yew Tree Lane were still in open country in 1902. In 1910 part of Palatine Road ran through fields. As late as 1930 Princess Parkway was a beautiful woodland area full of formal colourful flower beds and quiet charm. Princess Mansions, a block of 1930s luxury flats, was built nearby on Wythenshawe Road overlooking the park. Henly's Garage stood at the roundabout on Princess Parkway before Gibwood Road was built. The garage featured an unusual 'split mansard roof' and was open 24 hours a day. The garage was demolished to make way for the subways. Northenden Silver Prize Band, a church-sponsored band, the Coronation Cinema on Longley Lane and Northenden Amateur Dramatic Society provided entertainment. Although Northenden had escaped the clutches of the Industrial Revolution it lay on the edge of an expanding city and there was always the chance that something would happen to change everything. Finally something did happen. Wythenshawe happened.

Barry Parker's dream of a garden city gained a population of 40,000 in 1919–30, but no shopping, educational, religious or recreational facilities had been provided for its inhabitants. Northenden suddenly found itself swamped by thousands of neighbours wanting to share in its facilities. Shops,

Bringing home the hay along the River Mersey in 1904.

Ox-roasting, 1910.

schools, churches and cinemas were needed. The church school on Palatine Road, a council school on Bazley Road, Yew Tree School, and the churches of St Wilfrid's, St Hilda's RC (on Kenworthy Lane), the Gospel Hall (built opposite the old corn mill in 1897), the Methodist Chapel, and a Mormon church on Altrincham Road struggled to cope. Palatine Road grew into the main shopping centre as businesses opened and prospered. A new parade of shops was built at Moor End. The Forum cinema opened on Wythenshawe Road in 1934 and the ABC cinema opened on Hollyhedge Road in 1939. The Forum had a Wurlitzer organ and a restaurant. The building still exists and became a Kingdom Hall for Jehovah's Witnesses in 1976. There was even a film studio on Palatine Road. The Rosemary Festival was inaugurated in 1934 by Rotary and local traders to raise money for charity while providing a colourful spectacle for onlookers, and during the 1950s Whit Walks were held. Wythenshawe was incorporated by

Ploughing in a heavy frost on 14 November 1933.

The old village in 1912.

A timbered cottage on Wythenshawe Road near Button Lane, Baguley, on 5 September 1944.

Manchester in 1931, dragging with it the areas of Northenden, Baguley and Northenden Etchells.

However, all this development was resented by the residents of Northenden who didn't want their village despoiled in this manner, but they were powerless to defeat the relentless cycle of supply and demand. It took over three decades but they finally got their wish. Wythenshawe gained its own shopping centre, the Civic Centre and the Forum. In 1965 Northenden railway station closed. With the coming of the motorways Northenden was bypassed and left to itself once more. The once peaceful Princess Mansions luxury flats were demolished and replaced by the Post House hotel in 1971. A modern Open University building stands opposite the Mormon Church on Altrincham Road. The whole area became part of Mersey Valley Park in the 1980s and since 1991 the population has remained static at around 12,500. Some of the old village community spirit is re-emerging, but the proximity and influence of Wythenshawe still provokes resentment and, on occasion, fierce argument. Northenden's air of rural charm and tranquillity has been lost forever.

Further reading:
Deakin, Derrick *Northenden* Willow Publishing, 1983

Openshaw

Openshaw is first mentioned in 1282 (during the period when the Collegiate Church charters were being drawn up), as Opinschawe. The name means an open or unenclosed wood. It was then part of the Salford Hundred, which came under the jurisdiction of the Manchester lord of the manor. Openshaw is said to have been 'an ancient wooded area, probably cleared around 1600' and 'about 1276 Robert Grelley (the then lord of the manor of Manchester) had a park there'. Park in that context probably doesn't mean what people today would consider to be a park, with formal gardens and provision of recreational activities. It would be a delineated area in which Robert Grelley had hunting rights (usually held by the king) to hunt game, such as deer and wild boar, and perhaps a hunting lodge where he could entertain his friends during hunting expeditions.

It is most likely that the woodlands were gradually cleared for farming and obtaining building materials from the 14th century onwards; perhaps more particularly during Tudor times when foreign policy dictated that England needed a sizeable navy and the huge warships took their toll on wood supplies. New trees would have been planted to replace those cut down, but England was a sheep breeding country at this time and sheep love the bark of saplings and young trees. The sheep were just as responsible as the Tudor monarchs for the decline of English woodlands.

A working forge and machinery in 1890.

In 1322 the *Survey of the Manor of Manchester* makes a statement, in flowery language with idiosyncratic spelling, of local facilities, annual depreciation and public rights:

> ...there is there the mill of Mamcestre running by the water of the Irk... to which all the burgesses and all the tenants of the town of Mamcestre with hamlets of Ardwicke, Oponshaghe (Openshaw), Curmesalle (Crumpsall), Moston, Nuthurst... and Ancottes ought to grind their grain to the sixteenth grain... (some to be left behind as payment for the miller)... of Oponshaghe

there are 100 acres of turf moor of the lord's soil which cannot be extended to a yearly profit because its worth decreases yearly so that it will be quickly annihilated; in which the lord's tenants of Gorton, Oponsghaghe, Ardwycke and the lord of Ancotes, have common of turbary (right to dig turf).

By the 18th century Openshaw was still essentially an agricultural area but a cottage industry of bleaching had grown up there, as in some of the more northern suburbs like Harpurhey and Collyhurst. Openshaw, sandwiched between Ashton Old Road and Gorton, was too close to the cotton mills of Ancoats and Ardwick, and to the newly-built Manchester and Ashton-under-Lyne Canal, to escape the tentacles of the Industrial Revolution. Engineering works and ordnance (gun) manufacture replaced the cottage bleaching industry. Beyer Peacock locomotive builders, otherwise known as Gorton Tank, covered a 12-acre site in nearby Gorton and employed hundreds of local workers. Gorton and Openshaw shared a railway station during the 19th century. Openshaw was officially declared an ecclesiastical parish in 1844. St Barnabas's Church had opened in 1839, followed by St Clement's in Higher Openshaw in around 1874. St Clement's School was built close by. New shops, including the renowned and bizarrely named Blatter's Bazaar, opened on Ashton Old Road and in Lower Openshaw, and there was an open-air market. Between 1821 and 1881 the population of Openshaw multiplied 32.5 times from 497 to 16,153. It was nothing short of a population explosion and in 1890 Openshaw was incorporated with Manchester.

Clayton Street. The bridge over Ashton-under-Lyne canal on 3 August 1900.

The inhabitants of Openshaw needed light-hearted respite from their labours. The Metropole Theatre (on Wesley Street) had been built by William Broadhead in 1899 'to provide dramatic productions of an uplifting and moral character at a reasonable price for this poor district'. When this idea resulted in a distinct lack of enthusiasm among the inhabitants, the local paper gleefully reported 'entertainment of a more cheerful kind, like Casey's Court and The Mumming Birds' coupled in 1910 with '... Dr Walford Bodie, a magician and bone setter, who cured an Openshaw girl of 11 who had been born a cripple...' There was also Hart's Theatre on Grey Mare Lane (superseded by the Princess Picture house which was later built on the site), where 'one Friday night a whole sheep was cut up on the stage and the joints given to the first twelve people to enter the theatre' (which caused much jostling since the door was only opened halfway); the Alhambra, where 'the Great Lafayette' played in August 1914 to an audience of 9,000 people, followed the next week by the quaintly named 'Cap'n Kettle'; the Rex Picture House and the Whitehall Cinema on Old Lane which, in January 1914, was showing *A Message from Mars* and *Wild Beasts at Large*.

During the spring of 1914 the *Gorton and Openshaw Reporter* cheerfully ranted under the heading 'Teachers and the Cinema' that

> ...under present conditions in this country there is no doubt they serve no real educational purpose... it is probable also that both physical and moral evils result from unrestrained attendance at these shows... two of the reasons given... pupils think less of cruelty, lying, deception, and even theft... the boys will steal to obtain 3d for admission.

There were also bitter complaints that the 'young men of the present day (are) worse than Nero... (with) their absorbing interest in football... Nearly 90 years later the jury is still out in both cases.

The Alhambra Theatre in 1912.

Despite brief respites, life in Openshaw was dirty, grim and hard. Business was still booming and Armstrong Whitworth, the Openshaw gun works, were reported 'very busy' in April 1910; but there was growing concern over 'the thick black smoke' from the factories. There was a deep desire by workers to improve their lot and Socialism flourished. Openshaw Socialists met at Old Lane and in June 1910 Keir Hardie, the founder of the modern Labour Party, gave them a rousing speech at the Whitworth Hall. Mr J.E. Sutton won the Gorton and Openshaw seat for Labour in 1910 with a majority of over 1,000. Annie Lee, who became the first woman alderman of Manchester in 1936, cut her political teeth in Openshaw by becoming secretary of the Openshaw Independent Labour Party (the forerunner of the modern Labour Party) in 1895 at the age of 18.

World War One proved to be the beginning of the end for industrial Openshaw. On 15 May 1917 King George V and Queen Mary visited the Armstrong Whitworth gun works, such was the output from

Millscape and the railway near Denslip Street in 1964.

that factory for the war effort. Less than two years later, on 5 April 1919, Armstrong Whitworth closed down. This resulted in 3,501 men and 7,488 women (from a population of 30,000) being thrown out of work. Unemployment queues stretched for 50 yards down Ashton Old Road and George Street in Openshaw. The unemployment problem was made worse by soldiers returning to civilian life. The reaction of many people was to drown their sorrows, and by May the local pubs were running dry. There were riots in Lower Openshaw over the 'no beer' announcement. Windows were smashed and publicans assaulted. There was a brief respite in August as people briefly forgot their troubles and joined in the local Wakes celebrations while the laughter of children could be heard at the Punch and Judy shows on the recreation ground in Delamere Street, but after that Openshaw found that its feet were firmly on a slippery slide.

Today the population of Openshaw is less than a third of what it was in 1920. There is little industry and the area is run down. The hustle and bustle has long gone, as have the factories, the theatres/cinemas and many of the shops. However, Openshaw is on the edge of the East Manchester Regeneration Scheme. It will benefit from the new businesses and new building schemes being brought to East Manchester as well as from the Commonwealth Games in 2002.

Further reading:
http://ds.dial.pipex.com/david.ratcliffe/lhg/vol2/openshaw.htm
Sutton, Les *Mainly about Ardwick* 3 vols, Manchester, 1975, 1977, 1981

Rusholme

Although it is not mentioned until 1235, the name Rusholme, or Russum as it was then called, is most likely to have been taken from the Old English word *ryscum*, a plural version of *rysc* meaning rush. However, the area may have been familiar to the Romans because a hoard of Roman coins was discovered by workmen in the 1890s at a point where the Gore Brook crosses Birchfields Road. There were 200 coins, dating from the third or fourth century, probably hidden at a time of some local crisis. It would have been the intention to retrieve them when the threat had passed but, for reasons at which we can only guess, the owners never returned.

Birch Chapel in 1840. The chapel was closed in 1844 because of overcrowding. St James's was built close by in 1846.

Five hundred years after the Romans had left, Russum found itself facing another crisis. The Vikings, much-feared Danish sea warriors, were attacking the country. The Nico Ditch is a ninth-century defensive earthwork which was almost certainly designed to protect the small local Saxon villages from attack by the Danes. It stretched from Ashton Moss (now Ashton-under-Lyne) to Hough Moss (Chorlton); a distance of some six or seven miles. Part of the line runs along Old Hall Lane and Park Grove on the Levenshulme/Rusholme border. As the area later came under the rule of the Danelaw it has to be assumed that the Nico Ditch was not a success.

Platt Hall in Platt Fields has an intriguing history. Platt is a mediaeval name for a small piece of ground. Platt Fields were held by the Knights Hospitallers of St John of Jerusalem in the 12th century. The first Platt Hall was a lath and plaster building, although the exact date of its construction is not known. It subsequently came into the possession of the de la Mores who changed their family name to Platt. In 1625, the Platt, as the house was by then known, was sold to Ralph Worsley, a local merchant. His son, Charles, was a major-general in Cromwell's army and became the first MP for Manchester, elected in 1654. When Cromwell took the mace, the 'bauble' as he termed it, from the House of Commons, he gave it to Charles Worsley and ordered him to keep it at the Platt. It remained there for three months before Worsley was asked to return it to Parliament. In 1774 John Lees married Deborah Worsley, the heiress to the Platt estate, and built the present hall, a fine red-brick Georgian country house. Today it houses the Platt Hall Museum of English Costume. A statue of Abraham Lincoln stood in front of the house until 1986 when it was moved to Lincoln Square close to Manchester Town Hall.

There was one other large house of note in early Rusholme. The earliest deed for Birch Hall on Birch Hall Lane dates back to 1190 and was granted to Matthew de Birches. The estate included woods for grazing swine and a corn mill and became the seat of the Birch family. Birch Hall, a black and white timbered manor house, was built sometime during the 16th century, though it is possible that an earlier house had stood on the site. However, Birch Fold Cottage (demolished in 1912), an old black and

Haymaking in 1900 at Platt Hall (background, now a museum of costume). A statue of Abraham Lincoln stood in the grounds.

A Rusholme Bakery van in 1900.

white thatched building, which was probably once moated, may well have been the Birch family's first home. Oliver Cromwell was reputed to have slept there during one of the Civil War campaigns. The Birch family later sold the hall and its estate to John Dickenson in 1743. Alterations and additions to Birch Hall in the 18th and 19th centuries almost hid the old black and white manor house and made the place look a real mixed ragbag of building styles. In 1926 Birch Hall, together with Birch Hall Farm and Birch Fold, was sold to Manchester Grammar School and demolished to make way for the building of the new school in 1931.

Birch Chapel was built in 1596 as a private chapel for the family. In 1697, Henry Finch, the nonconformist minister of the chapel, was deprived of his living by George Birch, who was an ardent conformist. Finch, together with his supporters, built Platt Chapel in 1700 on Blake Flatt near Wilmslow Road. The chapel was demolished and rebuilt in 1791. In 1833 there were gruesome tales of bodysnatchers leaving freshly exhumed corpses by the gravesides to scare Sunday school children. The chapel was altered and extended during the 1880s, but the congregation slowly drifted away as the 20th century progressed. It was finally closed in 1970 and the building was purchased by the Manchester Amateur Photographic Society. In 1753 John Dickenson had given money for a small chapel to be added to the main Birch Chapel. Despite the rival Platt Chapel, the congregation of Birch Chapel had continued to grow steadily. By 1844 Birch Chapel became too crowded and was closed. It was replaced by St James's Church, built about 20 yards to the east of the chapel in 1846. St James's finally closed in 1979, the parish then joining with that of the Holy Innocents in neighbouring Fallowfield to cater for remaining worshippers.

Several churches were built during the 19th century to cater for the growing population of Rusholme. In addition to St James's, Holy Trinity Church was built on Platt Lane in 1846 and a

Wilmslow Road in 1907. Today it is a fast busy road.

Primitive Methodist Church was built on Moor Street during the 1840s (although this had been converted into private dwellings by 1938). The Congregational Church was first established in 1839 as a Sunday school and then as a chapel in Kingthorne Grove in 1853. It was rebuilt on Wilmslow Road in 1864 and it was here that Herbert H. Asquith, later to become prime minister, married Helen Melland in 1877. The church was finally demolished in 1978. Dickenson Road Methodist Church (originally the Wesleyan Church for Rusholme) was built in 1829. The church had a chequered history. In 1863 it was rebuilt in Ladybarn Lane; the whole building being moved and rebuilt with two extra storeys added for use as a working men's club. It closed as a church in 1940. During the next two decades it was used as film studios, turning out a number of rather good comedy films which earned Rusholme the nickname of 'Manchester's Hollywood'. Afterwards it was used as studios for BBC Television.

Rusholme was agricultural until the 19th century, although during the 18th century cottage industries, such as spinning, weaving, shoe-making and rope manufacture flourished. Wilmslow Road was turnpiked in the 1770s and in around 1830 large middle-class houses began to be built in this area, and in nearby Victoria Park, marking the beginning

Norman Road fire sub-station on 29 June 1912. One fireman would be on duty 24 hours a day.

of the transition from rural economy to suburban residential. Ashfield House in Platt Fields Park had 'extensive pleasure gardens' in which were displayed some 15th-century windows removed from the nave of Manchester Cathedral during renovation work. Sadly neither Ashfield nor the windows have survived. Grangethorpe, built in 1882, was an ornate Victorian house of style set in ornamental gardens. In 1916 it was sold to the Red Cross for use as a hospital to treat wounded soldiers from Flanders, Gallipoli and the Somme, but by 1929 the Ministry of Pensions had closed the hospital and sold it to Manchester Royal Infirmary which, in turn, sold it to Manchester Girls High School in 1936. Other fine houses were built on Wilmslow Road such as the Oaks (now Ashburne Hall of Residence for students), Melbourne House, Birch Villa, Platt Terrace, Platt Cottage, Platt House and Platt Abbey. Platt Abbey (demolished in 1950) was the birthplace of the novelist and playwright, Ian Hay, who was born John Hay Beith in 1876.

The railway had arrived in the mid-1850s and was followed by the horse trams in 1880. From 1870 onwards house building increased dramatically and a few years later, the acclaimed children's writer, Beatrix Potter, noted in her journal that Rusholme was being laid out into streets. Rusholme was incorporated with Manchester in 1885. There was little industry, though the Co-operative Printworks stood on the corner of Hamilton Road and Stamford Road. Working class two-up two-down cottages were built in old Rusholme village around the Nelson Street/Nelson Place area between Platt Lane and Clairmont Road. Another famous Rusholme son was the cricket commentator, Neville Cardus, born at No.2 Summer Place in 1891. He learned to play cricket on the Corporation rubbish tip and attended the local Board School, which he described as 'a place of darkness and inhumanity'.

In addition to the Board School there was 'Little Birch', the infants school opposite Stanley Avenue (1846–); 'Big Birch', which was Birch School on Dane's Road (1841–1976); Chadwick's School (which closed when Little Birch opened) on the corner of Birch Hall Lane and Dickenson Road; and much later, St James's C of E Primary School (1965–). Manchester High School for Girls moved from Chorlton on Medlock to a new school built in 1940

The Nico Ditch, also known as the Mickle Ditch, at Platt Fields. The Nico Ditch was a ninth-century Danish defensive earthwork.

on the site of Grangethorpe. The new school opened in September 1940 but was destroyed by German enemy action on 23 December 1940. It was rebuilt in 1951. Manchester Grammar School, on the former Birch Hall Estate, on the Rusholme-Fallowfield border, was bombed in 1941 when the writer's father was a 15-year-old pupil there. The grounds and some houses in Old Hall Lane suffered damage, but the school did not close.

By 1900 Rusholme's days as a country village were over. In 1908 a splendid Exhibition Hall was built on the corner of Old Hall Lane and Whitworth Lane. It measured 600ft long and 216ft wide with a ground floor area of 100,000sq ft. It was the largest exhibition hall in England after Olympia but it was to be short-lived. In 1913 it was burned down by suffragettes as a protest on the eve of a visit by Herbert Asquith who was by then prime minister.

Recreation and entertainment in Rusholme were diverse. In 1877 Rusholme Real Ice Skating Rink opened on Moor Street close to the home of Doctor Melland, whose daughter Helen had married H.H. Asquith. The first library in Rusholme also stood on Moor Street, near its junction with Wilmslow Road. On the opposite corner stood the Trocadero Cinema. Birchfields Park was opened in 1888 on Birchfields Road (off Dickenson Road). As well as the usual facilities for recreational activities there was a bandstand for Sunday afternoon concerts. During World War Two the park was one of the barrage balloon sites designed to protect people from dive-bombing by enemy planes. The Rusholme Real Ice Skating Rink had closed in 1905 but during the 20th century Birch Park Skating Palace became well known. In the 1960s popular groups such as Brian Poole and the Tremeloes were performing there.

Dickenson Road. The BBC Television North Studios in a former Methodist Church, 1970.

Later it became a night-club, going under the various names of Oceans 11, Genevieve's and the Sting. The Rusholme Electric Theatre opened in 1910 near Harrods Depository on Wilmslow Road. Initially films and variety shows were offered but in 1923 Mr Belt founded the Rusholme Repertory Theatre and plays became the main form of entertainment. From 1940–70 it reverted to use as a cinema. In around 1980 it was briefly reopened to show Asian films, but was destroyed by fire in 1982.

During the last 30 years of the 20th century numbers of West African and Asian families arrived in Rusholme. There is now a strong Eastern culture in the suburb and, much to the delight of local students, some excellent curry houses. Many of the surviving larger houses have been turned into halls of residence for Manchester University students and the Owens Park complex has encompassed much of Oak Drive. The population has expanded by over 50 percent since 1991 and today, with a resident population of just under 16,000, Rusholme has a cosmopolitan flavour. It is very different from the quiet country village which Beatrix Potter saw being laid out in a street grid for expansion to a suburb of Manchester.

Further reading:
Helm, Peter and Gay Sussex *Looking back at Rusholme and Fallowfield* Willow Publishing, 1984
Mrs Linnaeus Banks *The Manchester Man* 1876.
Buckley, J.S. *The History of Birch in Rusholme* 1910
Royle, W. *History of Rusholme with gossipy talk of men and things* 1914.

Victoria Park

Victoria Park lies on the edge of Rusholme and is not strictly a suburb in its own right, but that is how it began life and for that reason it is being treated separately here. Its early history is indistinguishable from that of Rusholme, but it took on an identity of its own when an area of land was sold to shareholders and speculators in July 1839 for an exclusive housing development to be built. It was named Victoria Park in honour of the popular young queen. Richard Lane, an eminent and respected architect, was asked to design the new development. In his plans the park was to be based on three crescents: Park Crescent, Hanover Crescent (after Queen Victoria's family name), and a third unnamed crescent (crossing Laindon Road), which was never actually built.

Late in 1839 the administering company failed, and in 1845 a Trust was formed to carry on the work. Large tasteful family houses with sizeable gardens were built, set well back from the roads amid trees and much greenery. The park was completely walled and fenced in, each road entrance having toll gates and a lodge. It became a very desirable place in which to live and attracted a number of influential people whose lives and backgrounds made them the celebrities of their day.

Sir Henry Roscoe was a distinguished Manchester chemist who was knighted for his services to chemistry. The Roscoe Building of Manchester University is named after him. He was a tall, good-looking man who married Lucy Potter, an aunt of Beatrix Potter. They lived with their three children in Victoria Park. Beatrix visited Sir

Ashburne House (demolished 1968) in 1905, on the corner of Conygham Road and Oxford Place.

Henry on a number of occasions because, unlike many men of his time, he believed in education and professional opportunities for women, and he gave her a lot of encouragement in her scientific studies of fungi, arranging for a paper she wrote on the subject to be read at a meeting of the Linnean Society.

A near neighbour was Richard Cobden, a calico printer from Chorley, who moved from a fine house on Quay Street to live in the park. He was also an MP and he was instrumental, together with fellow MP John Bright, in obtaining the repeal of the Corn Laws in 1846. Other well-known inhabitants of the park included the artist Ford Madox Brown; Sir Charles Halle who gave his name to the Halle Orchestra; George Hadfield MP and Emmeline Pankhurst.

Ashburne House, built on the corner of Conyngham Road and Oxford Place in 1849, was home to Robert Barbour, who was associated with the re-foundation of Manchester Grammar School, and to William Romaine Callendar Jnr, who entertained Benjamin Disraeli and his wife there. In the early years of the 20th century

Lodges on Wilmslow Road in 1866.

Daisy Bank Road and Longford Place in 1907.

Ashburne House became a university hall of residence named Ashburne Hall. Subsequently Ashburne Hall moved to the corner of Old Hall Lane and Wilmslow Road. The former Ashburne House building was renamed Egerton Hall and became a theological college. In 1960 it was converted to flats but it was demolished 10 years later. The present building on the site is known as Ashburne House Flats.

The park had its own church of St John Chrysystom, built in about 1877 on Anson Road. In 1904 the church was destroyed by fire and a temporary iron church was constructed on the corner of Anson Road and Daisy Bank Road until the new church was rebuilt in 1906. Anson Road also had a golf course and a golf club for the use and enjoyment of park residents.

Lower Park Road. Ward Hall, Xaverian College Preparatory School, 1956.

However, Victoria Park's days as an area of select housing were numbered. Pressure from the city's growing population meant that building land was at a premium and the park began to lose some of its desirable reputation when new housing developments started to encroach on the area. The final body blow was the building of the Anson Estate on Anson golf club land shortly after the end of World War One in 1918. The main toll road through the park was made a free public highway in 1938 and toll gates on the

Anson Road, Dalton Hall and St Chrysostom's Church in March 1976.

side roads were finally abolished in 1954. Most of the large houses became university halls of residence; one or two became nursing homes. In 1976 Victoria Park was designated a conservation area by way of being an 'elegant anachronism' in the heart of industrial Manchester.

Further reading:
Bosdin Leech, Dr E. *A short account of Victoria Park, Manchester* 1937
Spiers, M. *Victoria Park, Manchester* 1976
Helm, Peter and Gay Sussex *Looking back at Rusholme and Fallowfield* Willow Publishing, 1984

Whalley Range

Whalley Range is a comparatively recent suburb and probably only known outside Manchester because Salford-born actress Joanne Whalley took her stage surname from it. The name itself is an enigma. The area was originally called Jackson's Moss and, as it borders Moss Side to the north-west, may well have been the moss which gave Moss Side its name. Jackson's Moss was the northern part of Hough End, which seems to have divided its time between being part of Withington and part of Chorlton-cum-Hardy. When Jackson's Moss was built up by Samuel Brooks in the latter part of the 19th century he gave it what he imagined to be the classier name of Whalley Range. Why he chose that name is unclear but he may have been remembering an old folklore tradition. Whalley is the Lancashire spelling of Whaley, which means a clearing by a road, and range is an old name for an enclosure, possibly using wooden poles or stakes. This begins to make sense because it could have been an old sheep pen; or, going further back into history (since *ley* is Anglo-Saxon in origin), because it was on a moss it may have had some sort of Celtic ritual significance. Alternatively Samuel Brooks, one of three calico printer brothers born in Whalley near Blackburn,

Brooks Bar in 1850.

Manley Hall, set in Manley Park, 1892.

Wellington Road, 1906.

may simply have named his new property after his birthplace. In 1834 he built Whalley House and named the road leading to it Whalley Road.

William Hulme Grammar School on Spring Bridge Road was one of a series of Hulme Grammar Schools founded in the north-west by the Hulme Trust, a charity originally endowed by William Hulme of Kearsley who died in 1691. The school opened in 1887 as an independent school, but in 1944 chose direct grant status until the abolition of this system in 1976, when it became independent once again. During the 20th century the school expanded and also acquired 16 acres of playing fields which back onto Wilbraham Road. Originally intended for boys, it is now a co-educational multicultural school. In 1997 Amberleigh Preparatory School was incorporated so that the school can take pupils from 4–18.

Whalley Range High School for Girls on Wilbraham Road (opposite the playing fields of William Hulme) opened in 1891 but has remained a single-sex school, although it has become multicultural, and takes pupils from 11–18. The school motto, coined in 1912 to celebrate the school's 21st anniversary is *Non Sibi Sed Omnibus* (not for oneself but for all) and the school encourages a sense of equality and community. The school runs its own radio station, Range Radio, and when the headteacher, Jean Else, was recently created a dame, the station celebrated this fact by playing *There is Nothing like a Dame*, one of the songs from the musical *South Pacific*.

There is great religious diversity in Whalley Range. Apart from the mosques and Islamic centres of worship, there are the Manchester Chinese Church and the Manchester Pioneer Centre for Spiritualism. St Bede's Roman Catholic College stands on Alexandra Road between St Edmund's RC Church and the convent; and the Cenacle Church of England lies on the corner of Whalley Road and Rufford Avenue near St Joseph's Hospital on Russett Road.

Whalley Range is bounded by Alexandra Park, Moss Lane West and Wilbraham Road, and much of

Lancashire Independent College (Congregational), 1928.

the development is in neat blocks on streets which follow a grid pattern, particularly in the Clarendon Road area. The Whalley Hotel was built on the site of one of the old farms in the area, Oak Cottage Farm, at Brooks Bar, which took its own name from the toll bar formerly situated there. In 1840 the farm was still flourishing. Nearby was the village pond where thatching straw was washed before use and in which vegetables were washed and cleaned before being sent to market.

Hartley's College (Methodist-run), Alexandra Road, 1924.

The suburb was never industrial and the ward profile of 1991 shows the lowest proportion of terraced or Corporation housing in any of the suburbs. Today there is a large multicultural population, centred on the area around Manley Park, which has enriched the life of Whalley Range and prompted the building of a fine new Islamic church on Wilbraham Road. Clarendon Road has a number of greengrocers shops catering for and run by Asian families and two of the houses have been converted into the Madrisa-Mosque Zakaria. Lancashire Independent College stands on Clarendon Road near Manley Park. There is an Asian International public call office on Wilbraham Road. Today the population is just over 13,000; a rise of nearly 5 percent in the 10 years since the 1991 census, about the same as neighbouring Withington.

Further reading:
http://www.whgs.co.uk/traditio.htm
Whalley Range ward profile 1991 Manchester City Council, 1993
Crofton, Henry Thomas *Old Moss Side* Manchester City Council, 1903

Withington

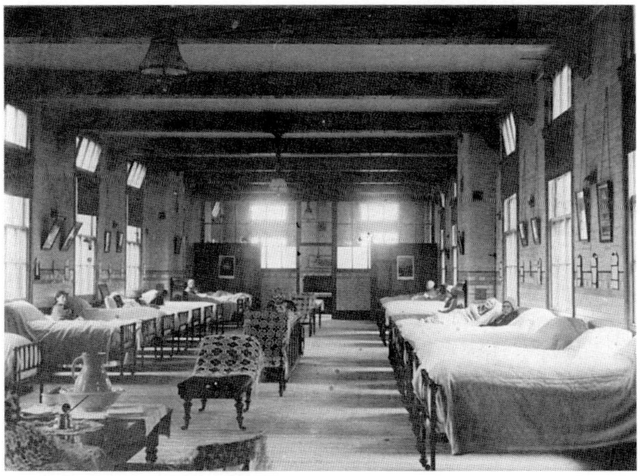

A ward for the sick in the workhouse, 1900.

Withington has merged with the village of Ladybarn in recent times and overlaps the suburbs of Chorlton-cum-Hardy and Didsbury. Sometimes it is hard to tell where one ends and another begins. Today it is a busy suburb and home to the internationally renowned Christie's Hospital and to the Holt Radium Institute. When the name Withington was first recorded in around 1186 it may have been just a single homestead, for the name means 'farm in a willow copse'. A withy is a branch of willow used for binding bundles. Ladybarn was a neighbouring hamlet lying on the edge of the Forest of Arden. England was heavily wooded until the sheep farming of the Middle Ages and the shipbuilding of Tudor times destroyed vast tracts of woodland. The area of Withington and Ladybarn was declared waste in the Domesday Book. This simply meant that it did not support any tenants of the local lord, no swine were kept, no honey was produced and there was no mill. In short it met none of the Norman criteria for a successful settlement.

In 1200 the manor of Withington covered a large area comprising Withington, Didsbury, Burnage, Chorlton-cum-Hardy, Rusholme, Fallowfield, Moss Side, Levenshulme, Denton and Haughton (both in Tameside). During the 13th century land in the area was granted to the Abbey of Cocker Sand by Odo, who was the son of Ingrith de Wythington. The deeds show the lands to have been to the south of the Nico (or Mickle) Ditch, the Danish defensive earthwork which runs from Ashton Moss through Rusholme to Chat Moss. The abbey was dedicated to Our Lady (the Virgin Mary) and a tithe barn was built in the locality which became known as Ladybarn. The small village of Ladybarn centred around Ladybarn Lane (now Mauldeth Road), Back Lane (now Ladybarn Road) and Arden Lane (now Ladybarn Lane), the main street. There were toll gates on Mauldeth Road in later centuries.

The Withingtons owned the manor during the 13th century; then it passed to the Longford family until its acquisition by the Mosleys. It is recorded that the countryside around Withington and Ladybarn remained largely unchanged until 1469 when the manor came into the possession of Jenkyn Mosley, a successful woollen merchant, who lived at Hough End Hall on the borders of Chorlton-cum-Hardy. By the time his descendants, Nicholas and Anthony Mosley, came into possession of the manor during the 1590s, it had grown to include Gorton and Heaton Norris. The Poor Law Relief Act of 1662 divided the manor into nine districts: Fallowfield, Gorton and Heaton Norris then deemed no longer a part of Withington. After the Mosleys fell on hard times during the 1700s, the manor was sold to the Egerton family, in whose possession it

Working farms in 1900.

The junction of Palatine Road and Wilmslow Road in 1910.

The tram terminus on Palatine Road in 1925.

remained until the early 20th century. Withington was incorporated into Manchester in 1904. Today the suburb is bounded by Derby Road, Lapwing Lane/Fog Lane, Princess Road and Kingsway; a much smaller area than the sprawling mediaeval demesne.

Withington was governed by a Court Leet (a court held by the lord of the manor) until the mid-19th century. Meetings were held at the Red Lion; the last being held in 1841. Officers of the court were known by various titles including Ale Tasters, Dog Muzzlers and Swine Lookers. Court records show that in 1592 a mob of 16 people from Withington and neighbouring Burnage murdered seven people from Moss Side in a dispute over cattle trespassing. The Red Lion was also the meeting place of the Withington Toll and Turnpike Trust in the 18th century. Mauldeth Road and Palatine Road were turnpiked and had toll gates.

On Wilmslow Road there was a public house called the White Lion. Just behind the White Lion

Home Guard Withington Company F Battalion, marching on 29 July 1940.

was a barn where the rushcart was prepared for the annual rushcart procession which took place each August. This marked the ceremony of renewing rushes strewn on the floor of the local church (before the days of central heating). Withington's first cinema, the Scala, was built on the site of the White Lion shortly before World War One. Withington had remained a rural farming area. Booker wrote in his *History of the Ancient Chapels of Didsbury* in 1857 that 'Withington had no mills or manufacture of any description, no colliery, railway, river or canal'. There is an amusing story from 1886 of a cow and a flock of sheep being driven through Withington. The cow, clearly wanting some diversion, decided to go shopping and entered a number of local establishments. Fortunately little damage was caused, but the drover excused the cow by saying that walking with sheep was beneath the dignity of your average cow and this had caused it so much shame that it had been obliged to protest in that manner! Maps as late as 1911 show Old Hall Farm (site of the original manor house); Oaks Farm; Pinfold Farm; Hough Farm and Yew Tree Farm, which covered 52 acres on Old Hall Lane (now Old Moat Lane). In 1871 603 people were working as live-in domestic staff against just 52 working in the cotton industry.

Times were changing however. The demand for workers' housing was paramount. In 1801 the population of Withington was 743. This had risen to 30,000 plus by 1901, peaked at 68,000 in 1951 and dropped to 27,000 in 1981. Today it is around 14,000. Corporation housing estates sprang up in Withington between 1919 and 1928, although house building had really begun in the suburb in the mid-19th century. In 1922 Old Hall Farm was demolished and 10,000 homes were erected on the former moated manor site. There was a commemorative plaque, bearing the coats of arms of the four lords of the manor: Wythingtons (1200s); Longford family (1300s–1400s); Mosleys (*c.*1469–1700s) and Egertons (1700s–1900s) to mark the provision of this select housing for the working classes. One of the first housing developments was the Albert Park estate built in the 1860s. Withington railway station, known as Withington and Albert Park, opened in 1880 on Lapwing Lane, and two years later a horse tram

The Christie Hospital and Holt Radium Institute on Oak Road in 1972. Both institutions are dedicated to the fight against cancer.

service to Manchester began. This was replaced by an electric tram service in 1902. The tram terminus was at the junction of Lapwing Lane with Palatine Road where a horse trough and a drinking fountain used to stand on the corner of Palatine Road.

Withington Public Hall opened on Burton Road in 1861 and it had a library of over 1,200 books. The post office and public library stood on Wilmslow Road. Withington Town Hall was built on Lapwing Lane in 1881 by Withington Local Board, formed in 1876, which became Withington Urban District Council in 1904. In 1895 the name of the area which included Clyde Road, Old Landsdowne Road and Cresswell Grove was changed to West Didsbury. One of the more bizarre episodes during this period of development occurred when a man named Ralph Waller built a solid wall right across the middle of Davenport Avenue in protest over a road maintenance dispute between landlords who owned property in the avenue. The rather splendid Methodist church was built in 1832, but the Methodists began the first day and Sunday schools in Withington in 1829. Other churches followed suit. St Cuthbert's Church opened in 1831 and the parish church of St Paul's opened in 1841. St Paul's RC Parochial School was built in 1844 and St Cuthbert's RC School was built on Palatine Road in 1891. There was also a grammar school on Lansdowne Road by 1883 and Carshalton High School on Heaton Road. Princess Christian College moved from Kersal (where the Manchester Races were held) to Wilmslow Road.

However, today Withington is best known for its hospitals. The forerunner of Withington Hospital was Chorlton Union Workhouse, built on Nell Lane in 1854, which had replaced the former Poor Law cottages in Lapwing Lane. Dr J.M. Rhodes, who was elected to the Board of the Chorlton Union in 1880, had worked hard to improve standards of medical care and treatment in the workhouse, which eventually became a hospital. The 'pavilions' of Withington Hospital, designed by Thomas Worthington and approved by Florence Nightingale, were built opposite the workhouse in 1864. A military hospital was set up on Nell Lane in 1917 to deal with casualties from World War One. It became known as the 'tented hospital' because it consisted largely of tents plus one of the pavilions. Today the site of the old tented hospital is Withington Hospital visitor's car park and Elizabeth Slinger Road runs across the site of the former pavilion. Christie's Hospital (named after Sir Richard Christie, a one time Chancellor of Manchester University)and the Holt Radium Institute (named after Sir Edward Holt, a former lord mayor of Manchester) stand side by side off Wilmslow Road built on land that was originally Withington Green, the centre of the former village. Christie's, which opened in 1932, is internationally renowned as a hospital dedicated to cancer patients and, together with the Holt Institute, has developed pioneering work in the treatment of cancer.

The star of films such as *Goodbye Mr Chips*, *The Thirty-Nine Steps* and *The Inn of the Sixth Happiness*, Robert Donat, the son of a Polish clerk, was born in Withington in 1905. The Withington he knew was a busy suburb but still countrified. Today, like all the other Manchester suburbs, Withington bears little relation to the country village it once was. The present population is around 14,000, a 15 percent increase on 1991. Lapwing Lane houses retain some very Victorian edifices, but there is modern building as well. Wilmslow Road is a fast busy road but grumbles about the provision of public transport have changed little since the days of the first horse tram. British Mountaineering have commandeered disused church premises near Christie's Hospital and in a very definite sign of the times the old Mercantile Bank of Lancashire has now become a health centre. The old traditions have long since ceased but Withington appears to be looking to the future with enthusiasm.

Further reading:

Hayes, Cliff *Didsbury, Withington and Fallowfield yesterday and today* Memories, 2000
Whittaker, Kenneth *A History of Withington* E.J. Morten, 1957

Wythenshawe

The quiet willow wood from which Wythenshawe takes its name, along with the sprawling country estate which belonged to Wythenshawe Hall when it was the seat of the Tatton family, has long since disappeared, to be replaced by a massive Corporation housing estate which rejoices in the name of a 'Garden City'. Until the 1920s Wythenshawe was very rural with ancient halls full of stirring legends and squat little farmhouses which survived through a market gardening economy. The area was sufficiently non-commercial not even to capitalise on neighbouring Northenden's 19th-century weekend trade of afternoon teas and amusements for stressed Mancunians who had escaped to the countryside for a day. Barry Parker, an architect and follower of William Morris, would change all that with his vision of comfortable homes custom-built for workers away from the noise and dirt and smog of the city.

Knob Hall, Higher Baguley, in 1895.

Of all the Manchester suburbs Wythenshawe is probably the one which bears least resemblance to its former self because of its sheer size (current population is more than 100,000, roughly the size of the city of Cambridge) and the growth of the Corporation housing estates during the 20th century. Other suburbs grew from a smaller, much earlier settlement with its own community and cottage industry. Wythenshawe did not, and like other settlements where there has not been natural evolution, it has struggled to find an identity. The establishment of three community associations during the 1930s attempted to resolve this problem and for a while they achieved some measure of success. In 1935 the Rackhouse Community Association was formed in Daine Avenue, followed by Royal Oak Community Association in 1936 and Benchill Community Association in 1937. The hall where the Royal Oak Association met was built by Noel Timpson of Timpsons Shoes. Benchill met at the Cedars on Woodhouse Lane. Civic Weeks were inaugurated in 1946 after the end of World War Two and in 1970 the first of the Arts Festivals was staged. By the end of the 20th century however, such community ventures were suffering from public apathy and sadly Wythenshawe was no exception. National government is now sufficiently concerned about the lack of community spirit to introduce citizenship lessons into schools in an attempt to reawaken some sense of community awareness.

Benchill Farm and ploughing 'Farmer Walker's Field' in 1895.

Haveley Hey Farm in 1895. Today a school covers the site.

Wheat-stacking at Benchill farm in 1900.

The Wythenshawe of yesteryear was a very different place. Rural, wooded, picturesque, tranquil, with no industry, except for cottage crafts. There are records of apprentices as websters (weavers), woolcombers, linen weavers and cordwainders (worker of leather). The only means of travel was a horse and cart; and, towards the end of the 19th century, the bicycle. Brownley Green smithy, or shoeing forge as it was called, was established in 1779. A wheelwrights yard stood next door. There were also smithies, or shoeing forges, in Baguley, Moss Nook, Poundswick and neighbouring Northenden. Moss Nook held an annual show from 1898–1913 at which the main attraction was a 'slow bicycle race'. The last one to reach home won!

The area was essentially agricultural with large estates for whom the local population worked. One of the oldest recorded buildings is Peel Hall. It took its name from the Celtic *peele* which means a small castle or fortified tower. The Celts were very active in the north-west and it is possible that there was such a building standing there once, but all trace of it has long since disappeared. Peel Hall was built in the 14th century as a moated manor house with a mediaeval stone bridge across the moat. There was an old chapel within the house, reached by a narrow oak staircase, which may have dated from around 1360 when Thomas Arden obtained a licence for an oratory.

Wythenshawe Hall, the seat of the Tatton family, was built as a moated manor house in Tudor times by Robert Tatton. There are records of a chapel

Broadoak Road, Walker's Pond and Lovers' Lane, 1910.

Wythenshawe Hall in 1920. It was the seat of the Tatton family and was built in Tudor times.

standing in the grounds until 1688 though nothing can be seen of it today. A tale of tragedy and passion was played out at the hall during the Civil War. In 1642, on 22 November, Colonel Robert Duckinfield arrived in the area at the head of the Parliamentarian troops. His soldiers smashed the east window of Northenden Church and the rector fled to take refuge in Ferry House, which stood on the banks of the River Mersey. The Roundheads then laid siege to Wythenshawe Hall. There was a fierce battle and six of the Royalist supporters defending the hall were killed. One of them had been engaged to a local girl named Mary Webb. She was heartbroken over his death. After two months of trying to come to terms with her devastating loss she determined on revenge. She took a rifle and set out to track down Captain Adams, the Roundhead officer who had led the siege of the hall. On 25 February 1643 she found him and she shot him dead at point-blank range. She made no attempt to escape the consequences of her actions. In her eyes justice had finally been done for her dead sweetheart.

Wythenshawe Hall was sold to Manchester Corporation in 1926. It is an impressive black and white timbered, multi-gabled building now used to house an art gallery and for conferences and weddings. There is a community farm and a large horticultural centre in the grounds. The farm sells home-grown beef, lamb and pork to visitors. Herbs, fruit and alpines are grown while the 'Safari Walk' offers rather more exotic plants in the form of banana, pineapple, tea, coffee and rice.

Magpie Cottages in Church Road on 13 April 1949.

The Tattons used Peel Hall as a dower house. They also owned Newall Green Farm, built around 1600, but rented it out to the Shenton family to farm. In 1757 the annual rental was £92.50, so it must have been a profitable place. Knob Hall, so named

Peel Hall, 1955. A 14th-century moated manor house.

because of the ball-shaped decorations on the gables, stood on Newall Green. It was rebuilt in 1681 and demolished in 1959. Kenworthy Hall was built in the 17th century on land owned by Robert Tatton but was demolished in 1974 when Princess Parkway was extended.

Possibly the most fascinating and enigmatic of the old halls was Baguley Hall, built in around 1320 by Sir William de Baggiley, who was knighted by King Edward I and married Lucy Corona, an illegitimate daughter of the king. Baguley derives its name from 'badger clearing'. The hall was a fine black and white timbered building with beautiful 14th-century groining and open trefoil work. Baggiley Manor is mentioned in the Domesday Book. The Baggiley family had acquired their wealth from owning salt mines in Cheshire. Sir William de Baggiley died sometime during the reign of Edward II. His daughter, Isabell de Baggiley, co-heiress together with her brother John, married Sir John Legh from Knutsford. Sir John was related to the Legh family who owned Lyme Park near Disley in Cheshire from where, so it is rumoured, the timber came to build Baggiley Hall. Edward Legh, the last male descendant of the Baguley Hall Leghs, married Elinour, daughter of William Tatton of Wythenshawe Hall. They had three daughters and the Baguley Hall estate then passed by marriage to Viscount Allen. The Mayer family were the last tenants before the hall was bought by Manchester Corporation. During the 1960s the hall became a timber store before being restored in the early 1980s. Today Baguley Hall stands incongruously in the middle of modern council house and concrete Wythenshawe.

Sharston Hall, the seat of the Worthington family, was built in 1511, rebuilt in 1701 and sold to Manchester Corporation in 1926. During World War Two it became the local headquarters for the police, civil defence and fire services. The village of Sharston (from 'shaw stone' meaning 'the stone by

Longley Lane, Sharston. The William Morris Press in August 1956, where William Morris's unique floral designs were printed.

the wood') was a quiet country village. A school opened on Sharston Green in 1800. A century later the school closed and became a tea room, which also held Roman Catholic, Anglican and Methodist meetings in turn. Sharston Tea Rooms became popular with day trippers because of its location and the good country teas served there until it was replaced by the Sharston Hotel during the 1930s. Ringway Road, Woodhouse Lane, Peel Hall Road, Green Lane, Clay Lane and Crossacres Road (all names evocative of their rural origins) were still country lanes and Bailey Lane was just a track across open fields. Sharston was quiet enough to have a Lovers' Lane, frequented by courting couples or, in the language of the time, 'those walking out together'.

All that came to an abrupt end in the 1930s. Sharston became the first of three industrial estates built to provide work for those who lived in the endless streets of soulless Corporation housing. Only light industries using electricity, coke or oil were established there in order to create a smoke-free zone. Trees were planted to try and preserve the rural illusion but this was brought to a halt by the advent of World War Two. However, as residents of Wythenshawe discovered to their cost, it takes more than trees to make a garden city. After the war industries diversified and commodities manufactured at Sharston ranged from biscuits through embroidery, hosiery and shoe manufacture to electronic equipment. Two more industrial estates were built in the 1950s, at Roundthorn and Moss Nook. National and international industries, as well as local ones, were attracted to the new garden city with a ready workforce. Roundthorn was home to Geigy Pharmaceutical (which developed DDT) and Associated Electrical Industries (AEI) while Moss Nook was chosen by Ferranti Automation and today includes the Ringway Trading Estate. Charles Geysin, the Swiss founder of Geigy, began his business by going round Lancashire on a pushbike selling dyes.

The years 1930–80 saw an increase in building in Wythenshawe. The population soared from hundreds to thousands. Wythenshawe's expansion incorporated Northenden Etchells, which did nothing for relations between Northenden and Wythenshawe. Etchells means land added to a village or estate. A dozen churches and as many schools were built in response to the demand. Sharston Shopping Parade at Moor End was demolished in 1970 to make way for the M56 motorway, but by this time Wythenshawe had its own shopping centre and market. In the early 1970s the Civic Centre and the Forum, which houses the library and a theatre of growing renown, were built. The Open University and City College cater for adult education. Much to its evident relief, however, the neighbouring suburb of Northenden, which had been forced to share its shopping facilities and public amenities with Wythenshawe during the years of rapid growth (by 1939 there was a population of 40,000 people and no public services), settled down to try and regain some of its former village community spirit; but there is still resentment of Wythenshawe and local estate agents privately admit that any property with a Wythenshawe postcode is more difficult to sell.

Wythenshawe Hospital also grew in response to demand from the local population. Baguley Hospital was opened by Withington UDC in 1902 as a hospital for infectious diseases on land belonging to the Baguley Hall estate. In 1904 the hospital was taken over by Manchester Corporation and used for treating tuberculosis (TB) cases. During World War Two the hospital was extended by the erection of huts to treat air-raid casualties and a military wing

Shadow Moss Road. This was the scene of the first fatal passenger plane crash at Ringway in 1957.

opened which housed a plastic surgery unit. The military left in 1948 after which the hutted area became known as Wythenshawe Hospital. Baguley Hospital reverted to treating chest complaints. During the mid-1960s a modern maternity hospital opened on the site followed by a new general hospital in 1973. There are now four hospitals on the original site with a total capacity of over 1,000 beds.

Manchester has the distinction of having the first municipal airfield in the country and no account of Wythenshawe would be complete without mention of Ringway Airport. The first airport in 1928 was on land which lay between Wythenshawe Road and Sale Road in Northenden. It was a temporary airfield with a Dutch barn converted to a hangar for the grand sum of £115. From here in 1929 the Lord Mayor of Manchester flew to Croydon to collect a temporary airport licence. Amy Johnson landed her biplane *Jason* on the airfield during her solo flight to Australia, and Cobhams Flying Circus gave 'joyrides' to the public. The airfield was superseded in 1930 by the opening of Barton Airfield on Chat Moss, but there was no room for expansion there so land was bought at Ringway for £80,000 and Ringway Airport was officially opened on 25 June 1938 by the then Minister for Air, Kingsley Wood.

During World War Two the airfield was bombed but there was little real damage. The first fatal crash was not until 1951 when a Dakota crashed, killing its crew of two. In 1941 a parachute training school opened for the duration of the war. Civil aviation resumed in 1946 and by 1954 a million post-war passengers had flown from the airport. The first passenger plane disaster occurred in 1957 after a Viscount crashed killing a total of 22 people. In July 1961, Yuri Gagarin, the first man in space, landed briefly at Ringway after being diverted from Heathrow because of fog. The first Jumbo jet landed there in 1970 followed by Concorde in 1971. Ringway parish was finally incorporated with Manchester in 1974, although Wythenshawe had been incorporated since 1931. Ringway continued to expand and in 1975 was designated Manchester International Airport. In 1947 the staff numbered just 12 but by 1975 this had risen to over 5,000. Today the airport has a second runway and handles over 12 million passengers a year.

Wythenshawe today sadly gives an impression of endless drab streets of Corporation housing interspersed by straggling industrial areas and bleak concrete blocks of amenities. The area suffers from problems in social behaviour and a lot of aircraft noise. Houses continue to be built and in some parts older and newer buildings sit uneasily side by side. Gone are the farms and fields, the agricultural way of life and the close-knit community that had sustained Wythenshawe for centuries. Gone are the country lanes and the hedgerows full of wild flowers and blackberries. There are still traces of the old willow woods along the M56, in Baguley Bottoms Wood and Gib Lane Wood, but old Wythenshawe, still in living memory, is just that. A memory.

Further reading:
Greatorex, Jean and Sheila Clarke *Wythenshawe* Willow Publishing, 1984
Deakin, Derrick *Wythenshawe: the story of a garden city* Phillimore, 1989